D1516616

AUSTRALIA FROM THE BACK OF A CAMEL

Adventures With Grandchildren

OTHER BOOKS BY ALLEN L. JOHNSON

Drive Through Russia? Impossible! - 1986

Canoeing the Wabash -
Adventures With Grandchildren - 1991

Biking Across The Devil's Backbone -
Adventures With Grandchildren - 1997

AUSTRALIA FROM THE BACK OF A CAMEL

Adventures
With
Grandchildren

Allen L. Johnson

Creative Enterprises

Dayton, Ohio

PHOTO CREDIT

Pages 62, 72 . . . . **Michaela Aquilies**
Pages 44, 47, 91 . . . . **Annette Barwick**
Back cover . . . . **Judy Holliday**
Page 83 . . . . **Kate McNamara-Kelly**
Pages 37, 52, 67, 94 . . . . **Lucy Rindo**
All other photos . . . . Author

FIRST EDITION

Published By Creative Enterprises
1040 Harvard Blvd.; Dayton, Ohio 45406-5047

Printed by BookMasters Inc.
Chelsea, Michigan

Manufactured in the United States of America
ISBN: 1-880675-02-1

Library of Congress Catalog Number: 99-94629

DEDICATION

This book is dedicated to my wife, daughter, daughter-in-law and grandchildren for their help and understanding in accomplishing my adventures. The author also wishes to thank the following people for their editorial and proof-reading assistance:

Lilly Bielak
Margaret Cotton
Gloria Johnson - chief editor and consultant
Karen Johnson
Don Swanson
Linda Keating Schwartz
Karla Reichert

CONTENTS

ILLUSTRATIONS

TITLE	PAGE

AUSTRALIA FROM THE BACK OF A CAMEL

Adventures With Grandchildren

CHAPTER 1

INTRODUCTION

"You want to take Kelsey where? Australia! Do you know how far away that is and how many poisonous snakes, spiders and lizards they have there?" my daughter Judy asked incredulously.

"Yes," I replied calmly. "We'll be careful and Kelsey can call home every week."

The genesis of the adventure occurred in October, 1992 when my wife, Gloria, and I visited Australia on a business/holiday trip. We flew to Alice Springs in the heart of the Australian Outback (desert) for the weekend. Driving from Alice Springs to Ayers Rock--the giant, red monolith--we passed Noel Fullerton's camel farm and saw a group of people setting out for a camel ride.

"That would make an unusual vacation," I commented to Gloria.

Not much more was said, but for the next year I thought about Australia and what a great adventure a camel trip would be.

I enjoy taking unusual holidays with our grandchildren. Our ten-year-old grandson Paul and I canoed 500 miles down the Wabash River in 1990. In 1992, nine-year-old granddaughter Tracy and I biked 600 miles from her home south of St Louis, Missouri to our home in Dayton, Ohio. To keep up the "every-two-year" pace, 1994 was the year to accomplish some adventure with seven-year-old granddaughter Kelsey. The camel safari

1

seemed like the perfect choice. I waited until Christmas to approach Judy and received the indicated response. Considerable discussion was required before she reluctantly agreed. Then I talked to daughter-in-law Connie about taking Paul and Tracy along.

"Sure," Connie agreed. She had successfully survived her children's two previous adventures.

Gloria liked the idea of a trip to Australia, but she opted to remain in Adelaide, South Australia and visit with the Handknitters Guild of South Australia rather than traipse across the desert on the back of a camel.

"I don't like smelly camels, I don't like the hot desert and I don't like sleeping on the ground," Gloria announced.

The where, when and how of the trip took a little more thought. Australia is as big and as varied as the United States. There are literally thousands of interesting things to do and fascinating places to visit. Drawing upon the experiences from my six previous trips to Australia, I started laying out the bare minimum of what I wanted to accomplish with several possible itineraries and schedules.

In order to get more detail on the center piece of the trip, *the camel safari,* I contacted the international information telephone operator in March, 1994 and asked for a listing of travel agencies in Adelaide, South Australia. The operator provided three agencies in alphabetical order so I contacted the first, Angas Travel.

"Yes, I'd be pleased to get you information on a camel safari, Mr. Johnson," Jodi Higginson replied with her strong Australian accent.

Angas Travel Agency faxed me descriptions of several possible camel trips. The fax turned out to be a very convenient form of communications. Not only did it give me a hard copy of the details, but it didn't require me to be awake when I received

2

the information. Australia is on the other side of the earth from Dayton, Ohio and therefore 12 hours different in time.

When I was a child digging in our back yard, my mother used to tell me that if I dug deep enough I'd come up in China. Her geography was a little off center. If I dug straight down from Ohio through the center of the earth, I'd come out in Perth, Australia--the same latitude as China, but in the southern hemisphere. When I was working during the day in Dayton, Jodi was sleeping at night in Australia. Therefore, the only time I could phone her office was late at night Dayton time, which was early the next day in Australia. However, I could send a fax at my convenience during the day. Jodi received the fax the next morning in Australia, did my bidding while I slept and replied by fax. Early the next morning I could collect the fax and peruse the details.

My plans started to consolidate by the end of March. While on a business trip to Copenhagen, Denmark in April, I called Jodi and asked her to book the camel safari for August 1st through 7th. She faxed me at my London, England hotel the next week with the initial details of the booking. At that point our travel plans included flying on thirteen different airplanes, to seven cities, staying in nine different motels, securing four rental cars, four coach reservations, one tour boat and the camel safari. A travel agent's job is not easy. I can only imagine how long it took Jodi to book and confirm all the different segments of our trip during the peak travel season in Australia. She did a wonderful job and as the travel industry points out, there is no charge to the traveler for the travel agent's services.

When I went over my initial itinerary with the grandchildren, they suggested we were planning too many days in the desert (thirteen days) and too few at the Great Barrier Reef (three days). I called Jodi from Buenos Aries, Argentina during a business trip and requested she change our itinerary to nine days in the desert and seven days on the reef. She set about changing all the affected airline reservations, motels, cars, coaches and boat tour.

"Your revised itinerary is all confirmed," Jodi faxed me. That lady worked magic!

Next, I made up a list of clothes the grandchildren should take on the trip. It would be winter in Australia--jackets and rain gear would be needed. However, we were also going to the desert and equatorial beaches--pack bathing suits and some cool clothes.

The feeling of excitement grew as we applied for passports and Australian entry visas, and waited for our magic departure date to arrive.

CHAPTER 2

GETTING THERE

Kelsey had never been away from her mother for more than a night and now she was going 12,000 miles away for 3 weeks. Judy had the uneasy feeling that she might never see her daughter again.

"I'll drive you to the airport," she said, wanting to spend as much time as possible with Kelsey.

At the Dayton airport, Kelsey, Tracy, Paul, Gloria and I boarded our United Airlines Boeing 737 jet on Wednesday, July 27th to Chicago while Judy stood by the window, waving, with tears in her eyes. After a smooth, 35-minute flight to Chicago, we landed and hurried to the gate for our United flight to Los Angeles.

"I need to see your passports and entry visas," the United ticket agent said. She leafed through the passports and handed them back one by one until she came to Kelsey's. She flipped back and forth between Kelsey's passport, her entry visa and her ticket, shaking her head with a puzzled look on her face.

"Is there a problem?" I asked.

"These documents don't agree! The passport has Kelsey Erickson, the visa Kelsey Holliday and the ticket Kelsey Johnson. What is her real name?" the agent demanded.

"The name on her birth certificate is Kelsey Erickson, but her mother has remarried and Kelsey normally goes by her mother's married name, Holliday," I explained.

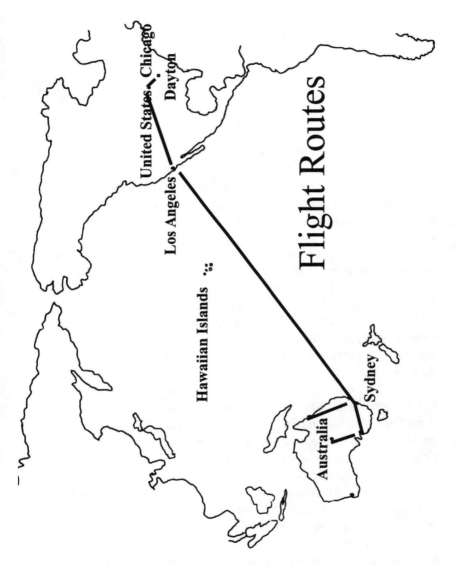

Flight route for Australian trip.

"And what about the tickets?" the agent asked.

"When the travel agent was booking the flight I thought it would be easier if we used Johnson since everyone else's name is Johnson," I explained sheepishly.

"Mr. Johnson, we don't change somebody's name on official documents just because it's easier," the agent replied. "And who submitted the wrong name for the Australian entry visa?"

"I did, but that was an honest mistake. At the time I believed that was the name she was going by," I replied.

"Mr. Johnson, this is highly irregular. The immigration agents in Australia will not accept these documents," she predicted.

Kelsey listened to this discussion. Her concern showed.

"I knew it! They're going to arrest me!" Kelsey blurted out as she stood in front of the counter shifting her weight from foot to foot. "I'm going to jail and I'll never see my mother again," she sobbed--tears streaming from her green-gray eyes.

"She's only seven-years old and this is her first overseas trip," I explained.

The ticket agent patted Kelsey on the head and asked her to stop crying.

"I'll let you go, but I'm not sure what immigration will do in Australia," she said.

With a sigh of relief, we boarded our United Boeing 757 flight to Los Angeles. I watched the movie while Gloria knitted, Kelsey and Tracy played cards and Paul slept. About 9 p.m. we landed in LA. Our 10 p.m. connection to Sydney was delayed two hours as international flights often are.

"Let's get some ice cream," Kelsey suggested.

After eating the ice cream, Kelsey lay down on the floor of the waiting room and immediately fell asleep. Paul and Tracy slept in their seats. Gloria and I stood guard over the children.

Around midnight California time, we boarded United's Boeing 747 for Sydney. Kelsey and Tracy curled up with two seats each in the center aisle while Paul, Gloria and I sat up in the three seats by the window.

I had brought along several books to read on the long flight, one being the history of Australia.

Australia is a continent in the southern hemisphere as big as the United States with a population of 17 million people. The Dutch claim to have first discovered the continent in 1606 (don't tell the Aborigines who have lived there for 80,000 years), but it was Captain James Cook in 1770 who claimed the country for Mother England. Having lost the American colonies in 1776-1783, the British started populating Australia with the first 1,000 prisoners in 1787. Many of the prisoners worked out their sentences and became the rich merchants of Sydney or the sheep barons of South Australia. Over the next 100 years Britain shipped 160,000 prisoners to Australia. The country gained its independence in a 1901 referendum.

There are many parallels between the United States of America and Australia. The original settlers for both countries came from England. Australia and the United States had gold rushes in the mid-1800s and wagon trains moving west. Each country encountered a large native population and built railroads and telegraphs across the countries about the same time. Australia and United States both provided a degree of freedom, unlimited opportunity and wide-open spaces unknown in Europe or the British Isles. Both countries are physically large and endowed with vast natural resources.

But there are also many differences between the United States and Australia. The Australian continent is the driest and flattest in the world. Their population is less than 10 percent of that in the United States. Australia is the largest producer of diamonds in the world, out-producing even South Africa. The

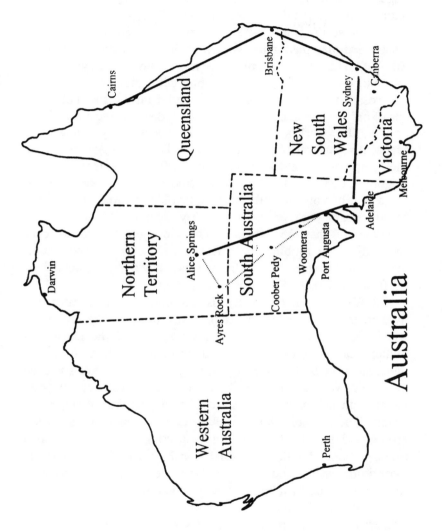

Route within Australia.

largest population of wild camels in the world, over 200,000, roam freely through the Australian Outback.

Australia is the home of bizarre and unusual animals: the duck-billed platypus, giant worms, sea-going crocodiles, and the wombat. The duck-billed platypus was originally thought to be a joke, like our jack-a-lope (a jack rabbit with antelope antlers), but the cross between a freshwater duck and a muskrat is real. It is one of only two mammals that lay eggs and suckle their young.

The world's largest worm, scientifically known as Megacolis Australis, is also real. The farming area near Melbourne is home for these giant earth worms that grow to lengths of 12 feet. The half-inch diameter worm makes so much noise as it burrows near the surface that sharp-eared farmers can hear them and dig them up before they escape. The worm is red blooded and has 15 hearts. The Aborigines used to cure rheumatism by rubbing the affected area with the crushed-up remains of the worm. Local farmers say they make dynamite bait for freshwater fish. All you need is a *giant* hook!

The saltwater crocodile is a 30-foot long man-eater that lives in the northern rivers leading to the sea. The crocodile, which was around when the dinosaurs roamed the earth 180 million years ago, has incredible patience and agility. It can lie underwater for up to two hours waiting for something or someone to come down to get a drink. It can then jump two-thirds its body length with lightning speed, seize its prey and drag it under the water. The crocodile can wrestle a full-size cow or horse to the ground and drag it off. Several unsuspecting fishermen have also become supper for this oversized lizard. Australia also has the most deadly snakes and spiders in the world. The venom from the funnel web spider will burn a hole in shoe leather.

A world renowned attraction of Australia is the Great Barrier Reef which runs 1,240 miles along the east coast from just north of Brisbane to the tip of Cape York Peninsula. The

Buildings in Adelaide could be from our old west.

world's largest coral structure is home to over 1,600 varieties of saltwater fish (including 20 varieties of sharks), 1,000 different shell fish and 400 types of coral in all the colors of the rainbow.

Opal is the national gemstone of Australia. They produce 90 percent of the world's gem-quality opal. One of the most productive mining areas is in Coober Pedy, located 1,000 miles northwest of Sydney, in the Australian Outback.

Sydney, Australia's largest city, was first settled in 1787 and today it is as modern as any in the world. The opera house is an architectural and acoustical marvel that is a recognized symbol of the city. The graceful Harbor Bridge (called the Coat Hanger Bridge because of its shape) connects Sydney with the north shore, Bondi Beach, and Sydney's Taronga Park Zoo.

Adelaide, the capital of South Australia, with a current population of 1.1 million, is a planned city laid out in 1836 with drawing-board accuracy. The architecture used in many of their buildings resembles our old western towns. The buildings in the business district look like movie sets from a John Wayne western. The center mile-square business district of the city is completely surrounded by a quarter-mile wide green park which housed the race track, zoo, golf courses, botanical garden and numerous recreation centers. Adelaide is connected to the Indian Ocean by a 150-year-old, 6-mile-long electric trolley line running down to historic Glenelg on the Gulf of St. Vincent. At Glenelg, the flat, sandy beaches stretches for miles providing spectacular swimming and picnic opportunities.

Perth, with its population of one million people lies, at the western side of Australia. It is the sunniest major city in Australia and is known for its beautiful white sand beaches stretching along the Indian Ocean. This isolated region would probably still be uninhabited except for the fabulous mineral wealth that the area boasts. Originally settled in 1829, the population boom began in the late 1800s and a 1890 gold strike resulted in more millionaires per square mile than any other part of Australia. To work their gold claims, enterprising miners contracted for a 400-mile-long aqueduct to pipe in the water necessary to separate the gold from the gravel. There was a big controversy about whether the pipeline was feasible. The chief construction engineer believed it was practical, but he had to fight a large group of doubters. At the completion of the pipeline, the chief engineer calculated how long it would take the water to reach its destination. The pipeline was opened and everyone waited. When the water failed to appear on the appointed day, the chief engineer committed suicide rather than face his critics. The next day the water poured out of the pipeline and generated the Golden Mile of Kalgoorlie.

We were eight hours into the flight when I finished reading. I needed to stretch my legs and find the toilet. These new Boeing 747s are marvelous flying machines. With all the innovations, such as winglets and more efficient engines, the model 400s can fly nonstop from L.A. to Sydney in $14^{1/2}$ hours. The original Boeing 747-100s couldn't make it in one hop so they landed on the equatorial island of Fiji after eight hours for fuel. While it's definitely more time-efficient to fly nonstop, my bottom can't endure sitting in one place for $14^{1/2}$ hours. I enjoyed the old schedule with a chance to get out and walk around in Fiji, breath some fresh tropical air and stretch. Instead, after 2 movies, 3 meal services, and $14^{1/2}$ hours of breathing dry, stale air, we landed in Sydney early Friday morning, July 29th. During the night, we crossed the International Date Line and promptly lost Thursday forever.

I presented our passports and entry visas to the Australian immigration official. Would he arrest Kelsey?

"Hope you 'ave a good stay in Australia, mate," the official said as he handed all five passports back to me. What a relief!

We passed through customs without a problem, rechecked our luggage to Adelaide and caught a shuttle bus from the international terminal to the domestic terminal. We raced to our gate and boarded the Ansett flight for Adelaide with only minutes to spare. Shortly before noon we landed in Adelaide--27 hours after boarding the flight in Dayton. We were tired--walking around like zombies.

We stepped out of the terminal into a pouring rain and 45 degree temperature--a definite waker-upper. I hailed a cab--compact Australian variety.

"I can't squeeze all five of you in one cab, mate," the cab driver said. Gloria, Paul and Tracy climbed in one cab while Kelsey and I climbed in another cab along with most of the luggage.

"Greenway Apartments on King William Road," I told both cab drivers.

As we drove through Adelaide I was impressed at what a comfortable town it appeared to be. There were block after block of well-kept homes, plenty of parks and green space, a river with people boating, joggers, kids on bicycles and couples walking hand-in-hand. It reminded me of Dayton, only bigger.

The cabs pulled up to a neat apartment complex on the north edge of downtown Adelaide. I climbed the stairs to the second-floor office to check in while the others snoozed in the cabs. I stepped over a big marmalade cat asleep in the doorway.

"Welcome to Adelaide, Mr. Johnson," the apartment manager greeted me cheerfully. "Don't mind 'Go Cat,' she thinks she owns the place. I trust you had a good journey?"

"After about 12 hours, the flight ceased being fun," I confessed.

"Well, let's get you in your apartment so you can get some rest. You're in number 10. It's a nice, big three-bedroom apartment."

And nice it was--all the comforts of home; three big bedrooms, a large living room, kitchen and bath. We dropped our bags in the various bedrooms and discussed how we should attack the jet-lag problem.

"The best way to recover from jet lag is to stay up until we can get back on a normal sleep schedule," I suggested. "Let's stay up until it gets dark, then get a good night's sleep and we'll be back on schedule in the morning."

"In your dreams!" was the universal response. Paul turned on the TV and everyone started unpacking.

At 2 p.m. Gloria lay down, "just for a few minutes rest." Right! She woke up 14 hours later. Kelsey was the next to take a nap--from 3 p.m. to 3 a.m. Tracy watched TV till she fell asleep at 4 p.m. Paul lasted till 5 p.m.

I walked downtown to Angas Travel to check on last-minute details and to meet Jodi Higginson. She turned out to be a pretty woman in her early twenties with a delightful accent.

"I feel I already know you after all the times we've spoken on the phone," Jodi said.

We went over our itinerary and cleared up a few questions.

"I really appreciate all the arrangements you've made for us. You did a super job, Jodi."

"Glad I could be of service. Please let me know how your trip turns out, Mr. Johnson."

On the way back to the apartment I stopped at a grocery store and bought cereal, milk, juice and donuts for breakfast. Everyone was asleep when I got back to the apartment so I went into the kitchen and fixed myself a cup of tea to help stay awake. Something started scratching at the kitchen door. When I opened it, Go Cat came strutting in, rubbed up against my leg and then walked into the living room. She jumped up on the couch, curled up and went to sleep. We later found out that Go Cat sleeps in the office while it is open from 8 until 5 and then looks for a "cat person's" apartment to spend the night. How she knew Gloria was a cat person I don't know, but for the next 10 days, Gloria and Go Cat shared the apartment. I fixed my tea, took it into the living room and petted the cat. When it got dark, I gave up and went to bed.

Everyone woke early Saturday morning. Tracy and Kelsey were awake first. Gloria woke a little later and made a pot of coffee. Paul and I slept until 5 a.m. We ate breakfast and repacked the clothes we needed for the camel ride from our big, hard suitcases into smaller, soft bags.

About dawn Kelsey, Tracy, Paul and I caught a cab back to the airport, leaving Gloria and Go Cat to enjoy the apartment. Two families we knew in Adelaide, the Mahoneys and the

15

Ramsays, promised to look after Gloria while we were away. She also had been invited by Margaret Cotton, the president of the Handknitters Guild of South Australia, to participate in their meeting.

We arrived at the airport in plenty of time for our flight so we ate a doughnut and drank some juice while we waited. Once we found the proper departure gate, the grandchildren and I played the card game UNO until flight time--Kelsey won.

Looking out the window of our Ansett flight to Alice Springs provided a good preview of how dry and sparse the Australian Outback really is--no big trees or grass, just scrub brush and sand.

It was noon when we landed at the Alice Springs airport. The bus took us to town, which is on the other side of the MacDonnell Range from the airport. As the bus passed through the mountain gap we caught our first glimpse of Alice Springs. It looked like a frontier town in Death Valley, California. The yards consisted of red sand or red dirt with an occasional tree, bush or small flower bed. The predominant vehicle parked in the yard was a four-wheel-drive pickup-truck covered with red dust. Most of the houses were small and weathered. A few tin shanties dotted the banks of the bone-dry Todd River.

The bus dropped us off at the Territorial Motor Inn where Jodi had booked us an apartment with four beds in one large room--no one had to share a bed.

"How long have you lived here?" I asked the pretty clerk as we checked in.

"I came up from Sydney four years ago. Didn't like the big city," she said.

"So what's there to do in Alice?"

"Lots of things. There are all sorts of neat tours, several museums, three cinemas, a casino, all the sporting activities and you can even take a camel to breakfast."

16

"We plan to take a camel to breakfast, lunch and dinner," I replied with a smile.

As we walked to our room, the grandchildren homed in on the hot-tub and pool. They were in their swimsuits before I set the luggage down. It was easy to figure out the best part of their day. "The pool," was their unanimous answer. They're easy to please.

They played and swam for an hour. I went in the pool for a short while to play tag, but they soon wore me out. It was supper time when I finally coaxed them out of the pool.

"Where do you want to go for supper?" I asked.

"Pizza Hut!" was the answer.

We ordered a large thin-crust with cheese and Italian sausage. Kelsey fell asleep in the booth while we were waiting and woke up only when she smelled the pizza. The grandchildren devoured it. After supper we walked home enjoying the cool, clear air of the desert and went straight to bed.

CHAPTER 3

MEETING THE CAMELS

I woke up shivering in the middle of the night. I thought to myself, *here I am in a motel bed under a pile of covers and I'm freezing. Tomorrow night I'll be sleeping on the desert floor. If I'm cold here with all these covers, what is it going to be like out there? Did I do the right thing signing us up for this camel safari?*

The alarm went off at 6 a.m. It was pitch black outside. "I'm still tired," whined Kelsey when I rousted her out of bed. Paul and Tracy just groaned as they rolled out.

"Come on, troop, this is the first day of the rest of our lives," I joked. The three grandchildren glared back at me in total silence.

We repacked, checked out of the motel and waited for our ride. At dawn a mini-bus from Jim's Fuel Stop pulled up in front of the motel. We tossed our luggage in and I climbed into the front seat while the grandchildren and six other passengers sat in the other three rows.

"Hi, I'm Jim," the driver said. "I had to drive up to Alice Springs for supplies and Noel asked me if I'd pick you folks up. It's about an hour-and-a-half ride to the camel farm so just sit back and relax."

"How long have you lived in the Outback?" I asked.

"I came up here from Brisbane in 1952 to try my hand at prospecting. Didn't find anything of value, but just stayed on.

18

Eventually I started a gas station and general store in Stuart Wells, and that's where I am today--40 years later."

Five colorful hot-air balloons drifted into view as we reached the edge of town. Each balloon carried three or four people in its baskets. The cold, still morning air offered perfect conditions for ballooning.

"Do the balloons take off from the airstrip?" I asked.

"No, that's the Outback Ballooning's sunrise tour," Jim explained. "They drive 20 or 30 kilometers west along the road that parallels the ranges releasing helium balloons every few kilometers. Then they watch the test balloons to see how the air currents are. They're very careful since they had an accident a few years ago and killed 12 people. Once they are satisfied the currents are right, they pull over and launch the balloons. The balloon ride gives the people a spectacular birds-eye view of Alice Springs, the MacDonnell Ranges and the desert. They even provide a champagne breakfast after you land."

We followed the highway from Alice along the dry Todd River and through Heavitree Gap in the MacDonnell Ranges. Once through the gap, the terrain became flat again. There was very little grass anywhere--just red sand and scrub trees. Occasionally we passed herds of cattle congregating around wells and dammed-up ponds.

"What do the cattle eat?" I asked.

"They go down to the water in the morning to get a drink," Jim explained. "Then they start roaming and grazing on anything they can find. They'll move out 10 to 12 miles from the dam during the day looking for grass."

"Lot of dead trees and brush," I noted.

"Yeah! We had a real bad drought back in 1973--killed most everything around here. In 1976 we were hit by a brush fire that scorched whatever the drought didn't kill. The area still hasn't returned to normal."

19

When we arrived at the Camel Farm we met a baby white camel.

Jim drove into Noel Fullerton's camel farm about 9 o'clock.

"Hi, I'm Marian," a middle-aged lady who seemed to be in charge introduced herself. "Noel is off on another camel ride so he asked me to get you started this morning. Put your bags down over by the truck. Mel will be driving out the back road to your camp so you won't have to pack them on your camels. Now, if you'll come in the office to sign the forms and pay the rest of your bill, we'll get you on your way."

After paying my bill, I walked out of the office and followed my grandchildren over by a pen that held a female camel and three babies.

"This baby camel is white," Kelsey called to me. "Isn't he cute?"

There stood a five-foot-high baby camel, weighing about 200 pounds. His hair was pure white.

"Albino camels are very rare," one of the farm hands said. "Worth a lot of money, especially in Saudi Arabia. There's only one other white camel in Australia."

"I've never seen a white camel before. Sort of looks like a ghost. He is cute," I agreed.

After everyone finished their paperwork, Marian introduced us to Andrew, our guide; Mel, the cook; and Neil, the camel handler. Neil had saddled the camels. As I walked in the camel pen, I was met by the strong, sweet aroma of fresh hay, the oily smell of saddle leather, the sweaty odor of the camels and the pungent scent of camel droppings. "This is going to be a real adventure," I said to myself.

Neil assigned us each a camel. Mine was Mick *(how much more Australian can you get?),* a light brown, 1,200 pound, 10-year-old bull. Noel captures wild camels, breaks them in and trains them for riding. Mick had been with Noel for about four years and was very gentle. Kelsey's camel was Charcoal, a small blackish-brown female. Tracy was to ride Jeda, a blackish-brown female and Paul drew Comanchi, a light brown, cantankerous gelding (castrated male).

Neil talked the camels down to their kneeling position so we could mount up. Once in the saddle, he gave us a one-minute tutorial on camel handling.

"If you want them to stand up, just say 'up'," Neil explained. "To get them to kneel, say 'oosh.' To make them go, flick the reins and say 'walk.' You'll notice that the reins are connected to a nose plug through a perforation in the side of the camel's nostril so be gentle when you pull on them. Camels are cud chewers and cannot take a bit in their mouths. To make the camel stop, pull back on the reins and say 'stay.' Turn them by laying the reins against their neck to turn their head the way you want to go. Camels are smarter than horses and if you're gentle with them, they'll figure out pretty quick what you want them to do," Neil said with a smile.

I gave Mick the "up" command and he jumped up like a shot, almost throwing me over his head in the process.

"We'll have to work on that 'up' maneuver," I told Mick.

After regaining my composure, I guided him around the pen testing out my "walk" and "stay" commands and the steering mechanism. Amazing! They really worked! I was worried about how 7-year-old Kelsey was going to do with her 1,000 pound animal, but when I turned to look, she was maneuvering Charcoal around the pen like a pro.

After a five-minute test ride, Neil opened the pen gate and our camel caravan started across Stuart Highway for the desert. When we were stretched completely across both lanes of the highway, a big semi-trailer truck came barreling down the road, hit his air brakes and brought his 50,000-pound rig to a screeching halt. The truck driver sat there while the guide, handler, ten tourists and three pack camels plodded across the highway, turned and started down the fence line at about three miles an hour.

We headed east across a flat, scrub-covered "paddock" (field) on a cool, windless morning under a clear blue, sunny sky. Our saddles were tubular steel and leather contraptions that fit over the camel's single hump. The basket area in front was where I carried my water bottle, coat, snack and camera bag. We sat behind the hump on a sheepskin or felt pad covering the leather saddle with our feet in the steel stirrups. Our seats were almost over the camels' back legs rather than being in the middle of his back as we would be on a horse. Because of this, we experienced the full motion of the hind legs. As my camel walked with his loping gait, I pitched forward and aft in a 30-degree arc like riding a sailboat through high waves. Some people become sea

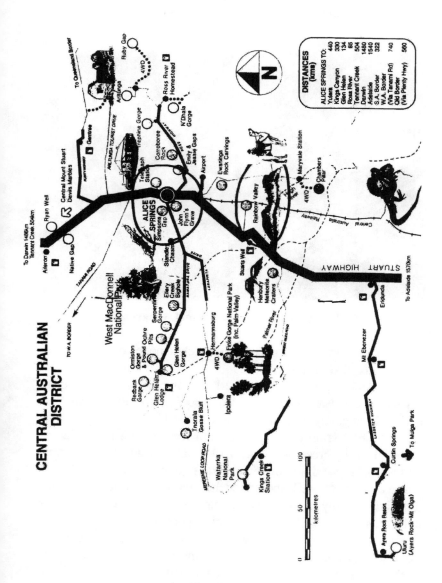

Map of Rainbow Valley.

23

Kelsey loved to run her camel, Charcoal.

sick due to this motion.   Fortunately, none of our group experienced that problem.

Andrew, who took the lead, was the picture of a relaxed, experienced rider: back rounded, shoulders drooping and his body rolling gently with the gait of his camel.

The terrain changed every mile or so from thick clumps of small bushy trees to rolling rocky hills, bright red sandstone buttes, open sandy plains and grass-covered ranges.   I was amazed at how well the grandchildren handled their camels, especially Kelsey. This 50-pound girl had complete control of her half-ton mount. Well, almost complete control.

Camels like to graze as they walk. Charcoal would swing his four-foot-long neck in an arc, taking a bite out of an acacia bush to the right of the track, some grass below, leaves of a whitewood tree to the left and then up to the ghost gum leaves

The Johnson troop, Allen, Paul, Tracy, Kelsey and Mick.

overhead. If he found something that tasted particularly good, he would stop and graze. To get him going again Kelsey would jerk his head around with the reins, kick him, and yell, "Come on, Charcoal. Walk!" If he fell behind, she'd hit him on his behind with her switch (whacker) and gallop him until he was leading the pack.

After about two hours of riding, we stopped to rest at a dry watering hole in a rocky gully. I parked Mick by a prickly bush and walked around to stretch my legs. Paul, Tracy and Kelsey climbed up in a giant gum (eucalyptus) tree to play. Neil and Janice gathered firewood and soon had a nice blaze to warm our hands and the "billy." Billa is the Aboriginal word for water. A billy can is a tin bucket used to heat water for "billy tea." After the water was boiling, Neil threw one handful of black tea in and

25

Tracy's camel was named Jeda.

let it steep. In a few minutes it settled to the bottom. We each dipped out a cup of steaming hot billy tea and good tea it was.

"Do you want an Anzac biscuit?" Andrew asked Kelsey after she finished her sandwich.

"No, thanks," Kelsey replied.

"Okay," Andrew said as he started to put the cookies back in the saddle bag. "They're chocolate."

"Oh, you mean a cookie," Kelsey yelled. "Yes, I'd like a cookie."

"We call them biscuits here. You'll have to learn to speak Australian," Andrew joked as he passed the cookies around.

After we finished our lunch, the boys and girls took turns making a comfort stop behind the big, red boulder on the edge of the water hole. Then we mounted up and rode on.

We passed up and down dozens of hills and gullies. The camels tend to trot down the hills. I had trouble getting synchronized with Mick's trot. I seemed to be going down when he was coming up. Very hard on my bottom, or "bum" as the Australians call it. Kelsey had her own unique style of riding down hill. As Charcoal started down, Kelsey would yell, "Ahhhhhhhhhh! Ow-ow-ow-ow-ow-ow-ow-ow-ow-ow-ow!" in perfect rhythm with Charcoal's bouncy gait. I asked her if it hurt, and she replied, "No." That's how she verbalized her excitement.

By mid-afternoon we were in the Hugh River Valley with the 2,000-foot high James Ranges on our left and 500-foot-high scrubby sand ridges on our right. The temperature warmed up from the early morning 40s to the 80s--a perfect day. Everyone peeled off their windbreakers and sweaters--some were down to their T-shirts.

Periodically Andrew or Neil would point out a wallaby or kangaroo standing motionless in the scrub watching us, or a wedge tailed eagle with its seven-foot wing span soaring overhead. The ride definitely wasn't boring.

We turned north into a pass that cut through the James Ranges. Thirty minutes later, a cluster of huge ghost gum trees appeared on the horizon as we exited the pass. They were actually white. When I rubbed my hand against them, a white chalk-like dust came off on my hand. Near the ghost gums were some dead trees where the Apostle birds had bricked up the big hollow opening with mud, leaving a small hole, just big enough for the bird to get in and build its nest.

We reached our modest base camp about 4 p.m. The camel camp consisted of a trailer for cooking and luggage storage, a saddle shed, a shower shed, two outhouses (dunnies), a small open-sided roofed sleeping shed and a camel pen. A small portable generator provided electricity for lights a few hours in the evening. Mel, who drove the truck, had arrived earlier and

This wedge-tailed eagle had a wingspan of seven or eight feet.

was in the kitchen cooking supper. Neil took all the camels to the pen and unsaddled them. Andrew issued us our swag and we each picked out a place to sleep. My granddaughters chose to sleep in the open-sided shed, a couple of people selected a tent and the rest of us opted to sleep under the stars around the eight-foot-diameter fire ring. Our swag consisted of a sleeping bag inside another sleeping bag inside a heavy canvas bag. We placed our swag on low cot springs to keep it up off the ground. Australia has more poisonous snakes, scorpions and spiders than nonpoisonous ones so the management tried to protect us novices, who couldn't tell the difference, from encountering an unwelcome nighttime guest.

Around 5 p.m. it got dark. We were there in the middle of the Australian winter and when the sun went down, it got dark quickly. Since there was no dust in the desert atmosphere there

28

We slept around an eight-foot-diameter fire ring.

was no twilight. It was either light or dark! The camp was lit by the huge bonfire in the fire ring, a gas lantern hanging from a tree and a couple of light bulbs in the kitchen trailer. About 6 o'clock Mel rang the dinner bell and shouted, "Grub's on!"

I was famished. Supper consisted of a huge bowl of steaming beef-noodle-vegetable stew and a butter-bread sandwich eaten around a roaring camp fire. Most of us went back for seconds. Mel produced fruit cocktail, biscuits (cookies) and hot tea for dessert. Since the sun was down, the temperature quickly dropped to near freezing. We moved in closer to the fire and sat there drinking hot tea and swapping tales of adventures until 10 or 11 o'clock. Annette's swag was directly under the gum tree. Andrew warned her to watch out for the "Drop Bears."

"Drop Bears are sort of like koalas only more clumsy," Andrew teased. "They're always falling out of the tree, and they thrash around as they fall.   Watch out for their claws," he grinned.

When I walked away from the fire, I was treated to a sky filled with more stars than I've ever seen in my life.   There were no clouds, dusty atmosphere or light pollution to filter the stars. The Milky Way was *so bright* it cast a shadow.   Alpha Centaurus, our closest star, looked as though I could reach up and touch it.   The Southern Cross led me to the South Pole, and Scorpio arched up directly overhead.

Everyone hated to be the first to go to bed because they were afraid they'd miss a good story or joke.   Finally about 11 o'clock I gave up, took off my shoes and windbreaker and climbed into my swag still wearing the rest of my clothes.   I lay in my bush bed and watched the stars for almost an hour.   The August meteor shower was in full force and I saw over a dozen meteors streaking across the sky.

Andrew piled several large logs on the fire before he went to bed to keep it burning all night.   I was so excited about this new adventure that I woke up every hour, stuck my head out of the sleeping bag and enjoyed the flickering firelight and the beautiful sky full of stars.   There were millions of them.   I watched the Milky Way move across the sky and finally set in the west.   The crescent moon came up about 3 o'clock.   The next time I stuck my nose out, Orion was just coming up.   He was upside down.   His sword pointed upwards from his belt instead of hanging down as it does in Dayton.   I lay there for awhile trying to figure out why.   Then it dawned on me.   Since I was in the southern hemisphere, I must be *upside-down!*   If I were standing at the North Pole my head would be pointed toward the North Star.   But if I were standing at the South Pole my feet would be pointed through the earth toward the North Star.   I finally convinced myself I really was upside-down and fell back to sleep.

CHAPTER 4

RAINBOW VALLEY

Now that you've met some of the cast of characters, I should tell you a little about each of them. The book jacket tells about me. Kelsey, the star of this story, is my seven-year-old granddaughter. She is curious, athletic, independent (her favorite expression is "I can do it myself, grandpa), intelligent and fearless. Tracy, my 11-year-old granddaughter by my son, is tall for her age, talkative, friendly and likes school. Paul, Tracy's 14-year-old brother, is an all-round outdoorsman--hunter-fisherman-camper-scout, very quiet or shy, patient and sensitive.

Andrew, our Australian guide, appeared to be in his 30s. He is athletic, self-confident, strong, talkative, unmarried, sporting a short dark beard and is a male chauvinist. Andrew is the nephew to Noel Fullerton who owned the camel farm. He loved to play jokes on the tourists, especially the women.

Neil the camel handler, is my favorite staff person. With his thick glasses, he reminded me of the small assistant coach, Herman Stiles, who acted with Burt Reynolds in the TV program "Evening Shade" in 1990. Neil weighed about 140 pounds, stood 5 foot 5 inches and was in his 30s. He grew up in Alice Springs and went to a school which taught mostly Aboriginal children. Neil worked with camels for years and then quit and went to Sydney to get married. He raised and handled snakes and lizards for a living and fathered a daughter who was then six years old.

31

Andrew helping Lucy with her camel, Bundi.

He recently separated from his wife and just returned to the camel farm a few weeks before our trip. Neil is very good with the camels and they respected him. He cares for them as if they are his children--brushing them every evening, fussing over a cut foot, putting salve on a spot that the crows picked raw, rubbing ointment on a saddle sore. Neil sleeps with the camels and talks to them all the time. He is a very polite fellow, funny, talkative and modest.

Mel, our cook, is a jovial heavy-set fellow who pretty much stayed to himself. He is interested in guns, hunting and motorcycles. When Mel joined us around the fire at night, he would tell stories and jokes. His cooking is excellent.

Lilly is a short, motherly-type woman about my age. She lives on a farm in Wedderburn, New South Wales, and raises sheep. She was born in Switzerland, married at 22 and emigrated to Australia. She has since divorced. I found Lilly to be a good conversationalist, an attentive listener, intelligent, kind and thoughtful.

Annette is our young, free-spirit. Her idea of a great weekend trip is a Harley-Davidson tour to Ayers Rock. She was in her early 20s and lived in Tasmania, the home of the Tasmanian Devil. She is petite, pretty, witty and liked to joke around and play tricks on people. She planned to work, play and move around for a few years to see what the world is like before settling down.

Michaela is a single lady in her late 20s, born in Austria. She is lively, sophisticated and intelligent. She works at a desktop publishing company in Sydney and is computer literate-- e-mail, downloading, file transfer and that sort of thing. She travels extensively and loves to talk about the sights, culture and history of Europe.

Lucy is a nurse from Tamworth, New South Wales, about 200 miles north of Sydney. A cheerful person in her early 30s, she loves to travel. She is quiet, helpful, had a keen sense of humor and sparkling eyes.

Janice is also a nurse, living in Blacktown, New South Wales, west of Sydney. She is a gentle person with a mature outlook. Janice loved to help out whether it was gathering firewood, cleaning up the dishes or getting someone a cup of tea.

Nathan is Janice's nephew. He was 11-years old going on 20. He is a very forward youngster who loved to tell dirty jokes. During the day, he usually rode up with Andrew and they would swap blue stories. Andrew has quite a repertoire of stories, but he admitted he learned a few new ones from Nathan.

I don't own a watch or carry a travel clock. Over the years I've developed the ability to estimate time with relatively good accuracy. By paying close attention to the sun, moon and stars I can usually guess the correct time within 15 minutes. For this trip I had checked the almanac and figured out when the sun and moon rose and set in Australia and when several of the prominent constellations such as Orion and Scorpio rose and set. In the early morning Orion was my clock. It rose at 3 a.m. and moved across the sky at 15 degrees an hour. A rule of thumb for estimating angles in the sky is, a balled fist at arm's length is five degrees. Orion was six fists above the horizon when I heard Andrew stirring up the fire at about 5 a.m.

Rolling out of my swag, I slipped on my shoes and jacket, walked over to the wash shack and splashed some cold water on my face. When I say cold water, I mean *near freezing*. Talk about a quick waker-upper--that did it. I hurried back and rolled a sitting-log close to the fire which was now blazing warmly. Much to my surprise, I wasn't saddle sore from the first day's six-hour camel ride. Not even any sore muscles.

Kelsey and Tracy slept under an open-sided shed roof--outdoors but under cover. They had opened up their sleeping bags and slept between them like blankets on a set of double springs so they could pool their body heat. When I woke them, Kelsey said she had been cold during the night. Tracy said she was cozy and warm all night. Paul complained that his feet were cold.

As they rolled out of their warm swags, everyone moved close by the fire to warm their outsides and poured a cup of hot tea to warm their insides. It was still dark when Mel called us for breakfast. The aroma of beef stew, scrambled eggs and toast greeted me as I filed through the cook's trailer and loaded my plate with a hearty trail breakfast. Food definitely smells and tastes better outdoors.

We rode across Rainbow Valley early in the morning to investigate some colorful sandstone ridges. The water had leached through the sandstone and dissolved the softest material, leaving odd honeycomb holes in the remaining harder material.

The eroded sandstone looked like fossilized dinosaur bones.

These sandstone honeycombs are not very strong and further erosion had broken off various size pieces--from small pieces the size of coins to giant ones the size of a camel. The broken honeycomb pieces reminded me of fossilized dinosaur bones--a backbone here, rib bones there and vertebrae piled over there. There were huge piles of honeycombed rock--red, white, pink and purple. It was eerie. In some places there were chunks of honeycomb hanging down like the spine of an animal with its head still attached to an upper rock. There were different shapes, colors and arrangements everywhere I looked. Now I understand where artists get their ideas for all the weird and beautiful free-form sculptures they create. The unusual shapes exist throughout the middle of the Australian Outback created by God and Mother Nature.

35

The grandchildren sitting among the eroded sandstone.

We stopped at one ridge Andrew called "Cricket Ball Hill." The soft, red sandstone ridge had hundreds of small round nodules laying at its base and many more sticking out of the hillside. I got off Mick and picked up one to examine it. The nodules were from 2.5 to 3 inches in diameter, the size of a cricket ball, perfectly round and of a harder sandstone material than the main soft hillside. Strange stuff.

After exploring the base area, Andrew led us up to the top of the sandstone butte for an overall view of Rainbow Valley. Spectacular! The hills were painted in a dozen shades of red, pink, purple and white; beige dry lakes; brown sand dunes; green brush-covered valleys; and black and brown dried stream beds--a rainbow of colors.

Neil started a fire on top of the hill and put the billy on for tea and biscuits. When the water was boiling, Kelsey poured

Kelsey liked her billy tea with plenty of sugar.

tea for everyone. After tea, Kelsey and Tracy entertained themselves by running up and down a 200-foot-high sand dune. Paul climbed around on the giant boulders at the side of the butte. Others walked around the top of the butte to enjoy and photograph the views in the four different directions.

The temperature started out cool in the morning and warmed up midmorning to a perfect 75 degrees with a fresh breeze. After our tea break, we mounted our camels and rode another hour to a series of sacred Aboriginal sites. The rocks in and around the caves were richly decorated with Aboriginal wall paintings and carvings. The ancient artists painted water bushes, wallabies, footprints, kangaroos, starbursts and snake-like serpents. Some people suggest the artists were recording a scene they had experienced while others believed they were trying to

Andrew showed us Aboriginal cave paintings.

influence nature to provide them with the bountiful scene they depicted.

While Andrew and Neil prepared lunch, we were free to explore the canyon, waterholes and caves. Kelsey wanted to see everything and in the process got tangled up in a bush with five-pointed burrs shaped like little girl's jacks. No matter how the burr fell, there was always a sharp point sticking up. She sat down to pull the burrs off her pants and ended up sitting in more of them. There seemed to be no way to avoid getting stuck while pulling the burrs off short of using a pair of needle-nosed pliers. It took me 15 minutes to extract the burrs from her shoe laces, pants and bottom. Kelsey was very brave during the encounter, never getting excited or complaining. After I removed the last of them, I shepherded her out of the area trying not to get tangled up in more burrs. The Australian desert can be a mean place. Did

Lilly led us down the steep rocky trail.

the Aborigines put the burrs there, like a barbed-wire fence, to protect their sacred site?

Lunch was waiting for us in the cool shade of a giant cave when we arrived back to the group. The grandchildren were famished and dove into the sandwiches, fresh vegetables and biscuits for dessert.

After lunch, Andrew led us up to the top of another big hill 200 feet above the valley. As we started down the other side of the soft sand hill, he stopped along side the trail to let me lead the descent. When I rode past Andrew, he whacked Mick on the rear end and my mount took off galloping down hill. I had trouble getting in sync with Mick when he trotted. When he galloped, forget it. No matter how I tried, I was coming down when Mick was coming up-totally out of sync. We came flying down the sand dune at a full gallop. My legs were flapping; I was

We crossed the dry lake clay-pan in Rainbow Valley.

screaming for Devine assistance and holding on for dear life. My
hat flew off one side, my canteen flew off from the other side and
my knuckles turned white as I clung to the saddle with a death-
grip. It was a spine-rattling experience! Miraculously, I made it
to the bottom of the hill still in the saddle. It would be several
days before my "bum" and nerves recovered from that butt-
pounding adventure.

"Go Charcoal" I heard Kelsey yell behind me and turned
to see her galloping down the steep incline like a stunt rider. She
wore an expression of pure joy on her face.

After everyone was safely at the bottom, we rode across a
large, dry lake. The four kids decided to run their camels across
the clay-pan at full gallop. I watched as Kelsey lay forward in the
saddle and held on. She rode as smooth as a professional, no
bouncing at all. Tracy and Paul rode equally well. The kids

loved to run their camels. Mick and I walked, as I nursed my sore bottom. Kelsey said her bottom wasn't sore, but she admitted that the insides of her legs were a little chaffed from rubbing on the saddle. I don't know if it's riding skill or weight that makes the difference.

Neil pointed out a group of dark brown rock wallabies on the trail ahead of us. As we approached, they moved 100 yards off to the side and studied us as we passed. The pint-sized relatives of the kangaroo usually forage for food in the cool of the early morning and rest during the heat of the day. Later we came upon a big red kangaroo. He bounded off to the side of the trail and sat motionless watching us. We encountered a total of five kangaroos that day. Kelsey pointed out some range cattle that were grazing at the side of the trail. We hadn't encountered any wild camels yet, but Neil mentioned he'd seen tracks of a herd of wild camels in the area.

We arrived back at camp just before dusk after an exciting day exploring the desert. I washed the trail dust from my face and sat down for a well-earned cup of tea. About dark, Mel called us for supper--T-bone steak, mashed potatoes, mixed vegetables, with pudding and biscuits for dessert. Everyone was famished and supper was delicious. Most went back for a second helping. I certainly couldn't complain about the food on this trip or the other arrangements for that matter.

Later we sat around the fire and burned half a cord of wood while we swapped jokes and stories--each person vying to top the previous one. Lilly related her solo drive across the Simpson Desert. The Simpson is a Sahara-type desert with trackless, shifting sand; few water holes and no people or accommodations.

"I wanted to do something adventurous just to prove to myself I could do it," Lilly said. She went on to tell how she set out in her Suburu with two five-gallon cans of gas, a map, five gallons of water, a bag of groceries, tent, sleeping bag, and a shovel. Several times a day her car became stuck in the drifting sand. She had to shovel it away down to the hard-pan to get traction.

"I just took my time and shoveled."

At night she would pitch the tent and stretch out in her sleeping bag.

"I could hear the wild dingoes howling at night. It was eerie."

One evening she came upon a camp and stopped. It turned out to be two oil rig workers who were traveling to Coober Pedy for water. She pitched her tent in the camp and spent that evening talking with them. After 4 days and 400 miles in the desert, she finally reached civilization.

When there was a lull in the conversation around the fire, I took Kelsey and Tracy for a walk to the dark part of the camp so we could see the stars. I had pointed out the Milky Way and other stars to the grandchildren when we were in Alice Springs.

"There it is," Kelsey said pointing up in the sky, "the Milk Shake!"

"No," I explained, "not the Milk Shake, it's the Milky Way."

"I knew it was some kind of a candy bar," Kelsey said with a laugh.

CHAPTER 5

BONDING WITH THE CAMELS

The Seven Sisters, or Pleiades, were *so bright* when I stuck my head out of my sleeping bag at 3 a.m. that the individual stars looked three-dimensional. An hour later I heard Kelsey whimpering.

"Grandpa, I'm cold!" she complained as the desert temperature hovered around freezing.

"Come over by the fire and get warm," I suggested.

I slipped on my shoes and threw a couple more logs on the smoldering coals. In minutes the fire was blazing again. Kelsey sat down on a log and snuggled up near the flames.

The water kettle was sitting near the fire. It was steaming by the time I got two cups and a tea bag from the cook's caravan. There's nothing like a steaming cup of tea to warm a body up. Kelsey added several spoons of sugar that turned to instant energy when dissolved in the hot water.

Our normal trail breakfast consisted of cereal, scrambled eggs with tomatoes, sausage and toast, in addition to whatever was left from the night before, such as beef stew. This morning, Andrew made the mistake of asking Kelsey what she wanted for breakfast.

"How about pancakes?" Kelsey replied.

"Pancakes!" Andrew bellowed. "This is the bush, not some fancy reee'sort!"

"Can I have pancakes, pleeezzzze?" Kelsey begged.

43

Paul's camel, Comanche, taking on water at the bore.

"Well, okay," Andrew softened under the pleading stare of Kelsey's soulful eyes. Andrew went into the cooking caravan and whipped up a batch of fluffy pancakes with hot maple syrup for her. Kelsey ate two of the plate-size pancakes and passed the remaining five or six to other hungry campers.

After breakfast, I walked down to the pen to check on the camels. Neil, who sleeps in the pen with the camels, was rubbing salve in an open sore on Mick's back.

"Did he run into something?" I asked.

"Nah," Neil replied. "The crows like to fly down and peck at the camel's backs. They do it out of meanness. They'll actually peck all the way through the skin until they draw blood."

By first light Neil had the camels saddled up and we headed out along a nearby ridge to a bore (Australian for water well) with a huge windmill. The windmill had about 30 blades

Neil took real good care of Kelsey and the other children.

stretching 20 feet in diameter. The unattended windmill was turning slowly and pumping water out of the bore into an open water tank where the cattle could wander in and drink whenever they wanted.

Andrew rode in first with the kids galloping behind. The rest of us trudged up to the water trough single file. Not all the camels wanted a drink. They only drink every three or four days. If they aren't thirsty, they won't take water. Camels obtain a lot of their water from of the vegetation they eat, such as the juice in the leaves.

Mick lowered his head to the trough and started sucking. He had a very long neck and made an audible sound when he sucked up the water. I could feel it flowing up his neck and rumbling down into his belly like a small volcanic eruption. Mick's sides amplified the rumble as the water poured into his stomach. Neil said Mick can drink 50 gallons of water when he is really thirsty. As he drank his sides bulged out and my legs extended out at a wider and wider angle.

"Used to have two windmills here," Neil said, "but had to take one down. Wasn't enough wind for both of them."

After the camels drank their fill, we continued along the base of the ridge. Andrew gave us a small section of rubber hose to use as a whip or as he described it, a "whacker." Tracy and Kelsey kept dropping theirs and since most of us tenderfoots had trouble getting our camels to stop and kneel down, Neil or Andrew had to pick them up. Tracy also dropped her jacket that morning; Nathan lost his hat. Andrew and Neil were forever backtracking to retrieve lost items. While he was retrieving Tracy's jacket, Neil gave us a demonstration of his riding skill, standing up backwards in the saddle as Fruba trotted along. He also did a headstand in the saddle. Neil was definitely an accomplished rider and acrobat.

A couple of miles down the ridge we came upon a huge cave that went all the way through the hill--in one side, out the other. This is the kind of site I would never see if I were traveling by car. We rode our camels up the steep ridge and into the cave where Andrew suggested we stop for an early lunch. Neil built a fire and put the billy on while Andrew produced some hot dogs from of his saddle bags. The kids voted that the best lunch yet.

While we ate, I asked Neil how the camels got to Australia.

"Camels were introduced into Australia back in the 1820s when the railroad and telegraph were being built across the Outback," Neil began. He went on to explain that the camels and their Afghan handlers were brought in to carry supplies across the inhospitable desert. Today, it is estimated there are 225,000 camels in Australia. Almost 200,000 of those are wild camels bred from those released 100 years ago when the telegraph was

Neil, the camel handler, showing of on Fruba.

finished. Australia is the only country in the world that still has wild camels. The last wild camels in the American West were seen in the early 1940s. Saudi Arabia has no wild camels and actually imports camels from Australia.

It is estimated there are about four million camels in the world--three million one-hump Arabic Dromedary camels and one million two-hump Asian Bactrian camels. Research indicates today's camel is related to a 12-inch tall rabbit-size camelid that roamed North America 40-million years ago. The camelids evolved into today's camels, llamas, vicuna and alpacas. About one-million years ago the North American camels migrated to Asia and Arabia. About ten-thousand years ago at the end of the last Ice Age, the last native camels died out in North America.

The pack camels were bred to be stouter and stockier so they could carry a larger load. They have a normal speed of 3 miles per hour and can carry a 500- to 700-pound load 20 miles a day. The riding camels have longer legs, a walking speed of 5 mph and can cover 30 miles per day.

The camel's anatomy is perfectly designed to work in the desert climate. They store food in the form of fat in their hump. A camel with a good sized hump can go for 30 or 40 days without food. Water is stored in their cells. To conserve sweat and energy, the camel can vary its body temperature, letting it rise as much as 11 degrees during the heat of the day and gradually cooling back down at night. That way, it doesn't sweat as much during the day or burn as much energy trying to keep its temperature constant. The camel can lose up to 40 percent of its body weight of water and still carry a 500-pound load. In contrast, if a person loses 12 percent of their body weight in water, they'll die.

Camels derive most of their water from the plants they eat. If they have access to green plants, bushes and trees, they can go three to six months without drinking water. When a camel has been stressed by traveling a long time without water, it can drink 30 or 40 gallons of water in 10 minutes. Within two days the water in its stomach will distribute back into the cells and the camel will be totally hydrated.

It takes about 10 to 12 years for a camel to mature. The average life expectancy is 48 years, and it can live up to 60 years. There is a collared pedestal on the camel's chest and four cellulose pods in the knees which it rests on. Bull camels can be very nasty during mating season. They fight other bulls for dominance over the females and will bite and kick each other to death in extreme cases. When a bull knocks another camel down, he will drop on it with his chest pedestal, bring his total 1,000 to 1,500 pounds down like an anvil to crush the ribs or head of his opponent.

Camels can jump, but not as well as horses. With training, they can learn to jump a three-foot range fence. Every year they hold a camel race in Alice Springs. Matter of fact, Bundi, the camel Lucy was riding, won the camel cup three times.

"A good camel can run 40 miles an hour for a short distance," Neil concluded as he packed up the billy.

As I mounted Mick after lunch, I realized the inside of my legs were chafed from rubbing against the camel while I was trying to hold on with my knees. My bum was also sore. First thing in the morning it felt okay, but by mid-afternoon I was wincing every time Mick decided to run or jump. My tailbone was definitely tender. The kids never complained. They loved to run--the faster the better.

From the cave, we rode up a narrow valley. As the valley floor became steeper and rockier, we tied our camels to a bush and walked.

"There are a series of water holes up this path," Andrew explained. "It is a sacred place to the Aborigines. Even in the driest season, there is water in some of these holes. They could always find food here too because the kangaroos and wallabies come for the water. To keep the women and strangers out of the valley, the Aborigines painted a Kurdatcha Man at the entrance to the valley to protect it," Andrew pointed to the rock painting. He explained that the Kurdatcha Man was the bogeyman or policeman for the tribe. He enforced the sentence given by the elders to anyone who committed a "crime" against the tribe.

We walked carefully past the Kurdatcha figure and up the path to the first water hole. The water holes varied from ten feet in diameter down to three feet across. The water was so dark we couldn't see the bottom, but the holes appeared deep.

One of the small caves we explored had been used by the Aborigines as a ceremonial site.

"The Aborigines inducted boys into manhood in this cave," Andrew said. "The elders brought their flint knives here and sharpened them on this stone," Andrew pointed to a granite stone with grooves worn in it. "Then they circumcised the boys at the conclusion of the ritual."

There were red ochre spiral paintings on the cave walls, kangaroo tracks, bird tracks and other geometric designs.

While we explored the next water hole, I noticed several one-foot-high ant hills between the rocks. There were thousands of ants scurrying along various paths. So many of them use the paths that they actually clear a strip through the grass which the locals call "ants' super highway."

Inadvertently, Kelsey stopped for a minute with her foot blocking one of the two-inch-wide ant highways. These were the type of ants that didn't go around an obstacle--they climbed over it. Before I realized it, the ants started running over Kelsey's shoe and some of them continued up her leg. When I first noticed them, there were about 40 or 50 climbing up her shoe and leg. These were not nice little quarter-inch-long harmless ants--these were three-quarter-inch-long black biting ants! I grabbed Kelsey and lifted her off the ant highway and stood her on a rock. Then I tried to brush the ants off, but they didn't brush off easily. They actually hung on to her shoelace, socks and pants! I had to pick them off one at a time. While I was frantically picking and throwing ants off, one climbed up my arm and took a good-sized bite out of the back of my hand. It was enough to bring tears to my eyes. Fortunately, none bit Kelsey. I was afraid they would climb up her pants leg, but they didn't. In a couple of minutes, I picked them all off and we carefully moved far away from the ant hazard.

After exploring the water holes, we mounted and rode up the valley. I looked up. There wasn't a cloud in the sky.

"Don't you get tired of this perfect weather?" I asked Andrew.

"Nope!" Andrew replied. "I like the sunshine."

The temperature climbed into the 80s or 90s by afternoon. When we stopped, I always sat in the shade. The humidity was so low that the light breeze made it cool in the shade. To accommodate the temperature change, from 30F in the morning to 90F in the afternoon, I wore five layers of clothes: T-shirt, shirt, sweater, sweat shirt and jacket. Every hour I peeled another layer off until by mid-afternoon I'd be down to my T-shirt. As the sun set on our way home, I'd start putting the layers back on. By 6 p.m., the temperature was back down near freezing. The heat evaporated instantly in the desert when the sun went down.

We stopped for afternoon tea in a place called Spiral Valley. At one time there had been volcanic activity there. Large pieces of black and brown obsidian--volcanic glass--were scattered over the valley. We found dozens of geodes--hollow rocks with a layer of quartz crystals growing on the inside surface. While we drank our tea, Lucy took a group picture.

Nathan, Paul, Janice, Allen, Kelsey, Michaela, Lilly, Tracy, Annette, Andrew and Neil.

Kelsey usually rode quite far in front of me. She liked to run her camel and lead the pack. I was usually bringing up the rear of our 12-person group. As far as I was from Kelsey, I could still hear her high-pitched voice as she shouted to Andrew or yelled at her camel, Charcoal.

It was later than usual when we started back to the camp--near sunset. With no clouds or pollution in the atmosphere, darkness moved quickly in as the sun set. We were several miles from camp when darkness fell. It was so dark, I couldn't see the trail at all. Mick knew where we were going. I just laid the reins on the saddle horn and let him take me home. I couldn't tell whether we were going to step in a ditch, a hole or what. Camels have very good sight and good hearing--much better than humans. Their eyes are on the sides of their head so each eye can see almost 180 degrees--from the front all the way around to the back. If I wanted to get his attention, I didn't have to whip him-- just raise my whip hand and he'd respond. By the time we arrived back at base it was totally dark. Mick navigated by the stars.

Once everyone was back at our austere campsite, Andrew brought out his space age lantern. It consisted of a bank of solar cells the size of a serving platter on one side and a fluorescent bulb on the other side. He left it out in the sunshine all day to charge up. With a full charge, Andrew said it would light up the camp for 24 hours. The space age torch cost $300.

The kids were looking for a game to play in the evening so I took some coins from my pocket and we organized a penny pitching contest. I drew a line in the sand. We agreed on the rules--closest penny wins. First we played for the Australian Championship--Kelsey won. Then we pitched for the World Championship--Kelsey won again. Finally we played for the Championship of the Universe--Kelsey won that also.

As we ate supper, Kelsey asked if we were on the top or the bottom of the world.

"The top, of course," replied Annette who was from Tasmania.

"Definitely the top," offered Andrew.

No one argued so Kelsey was convinced that Australia was on the top of the world.

By the light of the fire, we took turns telling a bit about our life history and previous adventures. Lucy explained that she was born to Italian parents, the only girl among four children.

"My family moved around a lot when I was young. My father cut sugar cane in Cairns, grew tobacco near Inverell and ended up buying a farm at Moore Creek. I studied nursing after high school. Then I worked at a hospital in Newcastle and saved enough money to take a trip to the Solomon Islands. It was there that the travel bug bit me. I bought a Kombi van and traveled around Australia with my girlfriend on a working holiday. What a fabulous experience!

"After that, I moved to Sydney and worked on my general nursing certificate. While there, I took a trip to New Guinea for a great holiday, but also caught malaria. I recovered soon after I arrived back home.

"When I received my general certificate, three girlfriends and I headed for Indonesia, Thailand, Nepal, India, Sri-Lanka, Egypt, Jordan, Syria, Israel, Turkey, Italy and Switzerland.

"Istanbul, Turkey was a fantastic place to visit with all its mosques and beautiful buildings, but the Turkish bath was a most unusual experience. The building was all marble with a beautiful dome. There was a women's section and a separate men's section. In the middle of the women's section was a series of heated rocks that we could lay on while the steam floated all around us. After we had enough of the steam bath, we moved over to a series of wash basins around the outside of the room. There, Turkish women sang as they washed and scrubbed us with soft-bristle brushes.

"The big dome at the center of the room had small, round windows. The sunlight was streaming through the windows down into the steam-filled room like spotlights. It was really a fantastic experience--just like in the movies.

"After 18 months of back packing, I headed home and worked at a hospital in Tamworth to pay off my charge card," Lucy concluded.

Truly an adventurous lady.

CHAPTER 6

THE WITCHITY GRUBS

As I sat by the fire sewing up the three-corner tear in Tracy's jacket where she had run into a barbed wire fence, I marveled at the beautiful morning God provided us. There was a thin, red line on the horizon where the sun would soon rise. The silvery moon had shrunk to a thin sliver and Orion stood one-third of the way up in the sky. Off in the direction of Rainbow Valley I could make out a line of huge ghost-gum trees. There wasn't a sound to be heard except the warm crackle of the fire.

One-by-one the other campers came to life and joined me at the fire. A couple of people in our group lounged in bed, resisting getting up before dawn. I didn't like to waste time sleeping when there were so many new sights, sounds, smells and tastes to be experienced in this unique desert.

I chose Weet-Bix for breakfast--big Australian mini-wheats without sugar-coating; a good source of energy and fiber. Others opted for eggs or the stew left over from supper.

Mick was saddled and laying by a barbed-wire fence when we were ready to start our ride. I unhooked his reins from the fence, hooked my backpack up on the saddle and told him how handsome he looked this morning. He stretched his neck out and scratched his nose on the barbed wire. Mick was tough.

As we saddled up and started out on our morning ride, I marveled at Kelsey's riding ability. She sat straight-backed in the saddle holding the reins high just like a Spanish equestrian rider.

She was wearing her white, flat-topped hat, and Charcoal pranced along as though they were riding in a parade. When Charcoal galloped, Kelsey's blonde pony-tail bounced up and down perfectly synchronized with the camel's gait. They were poetry in motion--an angel with a whip.

We rode south past a stand of ghost-gum trees that looked as though someone had just white-washed them. Entering a small valley, Andrew signaled for us to stop. He led us on foot up the side of the hill to a fossil bed with 300-million-year-old trilobites, cephalopods and crinoids lying among the rocks. The grandkids found a dozen fossils and some other "pretty" rocks. Lilly, who is an experienced rock collector, pointed out some "Levitrite."

"What's Levitrite?" I asked

"That's the kind of rock that you ought to 'leave it right' here," she replied with a laugh. "I have a whole box of 'Wonder' stones at home," she continued. "I wonder why I ever picked them up in the first place."

With my fanny-pack full of fossils and rocks, we continued on through scrub brush. As we walked along, Mick would reach over and take a bite of a thorn tree, stripping all the leaves off without getting the thorns. Then he would take a big bite of a sticker bush, chew it up and swallow stickers and all. Camels are real eating machines with a tough mouths and cast-iron stomachs.

We passed many beautiful wildflowers growing among the weeds. One called the yellow-top flower had eight yellow petals. Another, called a poached-egg daisy, had a big yellow center and little white petals. There were also blue daisy-like flowers that grew on a bush. They had a dark blue center, light blue petals and a sweet scent. All the flowers in the desert seem to be small and delicate. As we plodded along, Mick stretched his neck down to eat a single yellow flower. Dessert?

Leaving the desert floor, our camels climbed a steep, stone-covered path to the top of a hill a thousand feet above the

56

One day Mick stopped to eat a single yellow flower.

valley floor. They are sure-footed animals, like goats. Their large feet have chamois-covered peds. At the top of the hill, we stopped and had a panoramic view of the desert--different in each direction: bush-covered plains, rolling hills, dry lake-bed and sheer sandstone cliffs. It was easy climbing up, leaning into the hill and the camel, but going down was a different story--a little terrifying. I tried leaning back, but I felt like I would fall off the back of the camel. If I leaned forward, I felt like I was about to tumble over Mick's head. As we zigzagged back and forth down this rock-strewn trail, I simply closed my eyes and hung on for dear life. To make it worse, Kelsey was coming down behind me yelling "ow-ow-ow-ow-ow" as she verbalized her excitement.

At the bottom of the hill we rode through a cave which was only about eight or nine feet high. Sitting on top of a big

The Aboriginal medicine man cut off his finger to increase his magic powers.

camel, I had to duck to avoid hitting my head on the big rocks hanging down. It was about 100-foot long and 30-feet wide with an opening at each end, dark and cool with a musty smell.

For morning tea we stopped in a ravine that had a series of water holes. Andrew built a fire; Neil put the billy on to heat. Andrew produced some delicious maple-flavored biscuits from his saddlebags to eat with our tea.

While the billy was boiling, we hiked up the ravine and found some Aboriginal wall paintings.

"An Aboriginal medicine man would take a mouthful of red or yellow ochre, put his hand up on the wall and then spit out the ochre to make an image of his hand," Andrew explained. "See how this one has a finger missing. You could tell which tribe he belonged to by which finger was missing--the little finger, big finger or middle one.

"Another powerful person in the tribe is the Kurdatcha Man--the policeman for the tribe," he continued. "He would have a little toe missing. The Kurdatcha Man isn't selected by the tribe and the title isn't inherited from his father. A tribal member dreams that he is supposed to be a Kurdatcha Man. When he wakes up, he goes out and gathers the feathers and makes himself emu feather boots, an emu feather breast plate and an emu feather hat--the Kurdatcha Man outfit. I've seen two authentic Kurdatcha Man outfits. They were identical--every feather was the same on both of them."

As we sat drinking our tea, I noticed several strange circular patches of grass growing nearby.

"That's spinifex grass," Neil said. "It starts out as a single plant and sends its root system out to generate a ring of new plants around it. The roots keep spreading out making the circle bigger and bigger. Then the original plant in the center dies. It looks like a kangaroo has been sleeping in the center because it is all crushed down and dead, but it's alive on the outside ring. That's just the way the plant grows. It continues to grow out until it gets to be six feet in diameter. Eventually the outer ring dies. Pretty soon the whole process starts over with a central plant sprouting from seeds."

While we were sitting there, a three-quarter-inch-long ant with a black and yellow body climbed up on my leg. I quickly jumped up and brushed it off.

"That's a 'piss ant'," Neil said.

"That's the kind that bit me yesterday," I recalled.

"You should see the bulldog ants we have," Lilly said. "They are bigger than that one and have huge pinchers. The pinchers are about one-third the size of their body."

59

After lunch, Kelsey took a 10-minute nap on Charcoal.

"Yeah," Andrew joined in the conversation, "a bulldog ant can pick you up and throw you across the room!"

"I laid my jumper (sweater) down on a rock one day," Lilly continued, "picked it up later and put it on. I didn't realize I had laid it on some bulldog ants. A minute later they started pinching me. I pulled off my jumper and blouse and frantically started brushing those ants off me. When I finally got rid of them, I had a series of bruises from my shoulder clear down to my waist where the ants had pinched me. They have venom that they inject when they pinch. It really stung, but apparently I became immune to it after a while because I've been bitten a number of times since. The later bites didn't swell up or sting as much as the first ones did."

While riding after lunch, Kelsey periodically leaned forward in the saddle, lay on her saddle bag and took a 10-minute nap. Charcoal obediently followed the other camels while Kelsey dozed, bobbing back and forth. When she woke up, she would go screaming up to the front of the line whooping and hollering with her batteries fully recharged.

When we stopped for afternoon tea, Paul, Tracy, Kelsey and Nathan climbed up a limestone wall to a cave. Lilly said it made her very nervous to watch the young kids climbing around on the rocks, but that's what kids do. These rocks were perfect for climbing. They consisted of a series of sediment layers with natural steps and hand holds. It wasn't like climbing a sheer granite cliff.

While we drank our tea, Lucy spied a spider under the rock where Neil was sitting. The two-inches diameter spider was right between his legs under the rock. Neil got up cautiously and moved away. Paul and Nathan picked up sticks and tried to coax the spider out. It apparently tired of the game and disappeared. Everyone else got up at that point and checked to see if it had moved to their rock.

When we started out after tea, Neil announced we were in for a real treat--he saw some witchity bushes ahead. We parked our camels and climbed up to the witchity bushes, stopping along the way so Neil could cut a digging stick. The witchity bush was about 10-feet high and 15-feet in diameter with a series of roots that ran out in all directions. Neil peeled the bark off his Aboriginal digging stick and sharpened the end to a point. He then knelt down and started digging in the dry, sandy soil a couple of feet from the base of the bush.

"The young witchity grub digs down from the surface and bores its way into a root," he explained as he dug deeper and deeper. Kelsey was right up alongside Neil staring down in the hole.

"Then it hollows out a chamber in the center of the root. It lays in the chamber and eats the sap that flows through the root.

Kelsey supervised Neil as he dug up a witchity grub root.

When it matures, it lays its eggs in the root so the next generations of witchity grubs can live there. The root will develop a distinctive bulge where the grub lives."

On cue, Neil uncovered a large root with a definite bulge. After considerable pulling, tugging and creative cussing, he finally broke a section loose. He held up the two-inch-diameter root and pointed to the one-inch hole in the middle. As I looked down the hole, I imagined I could see the beady eyes of a witchity grub looking back at me.

"Witchity grubs don't have eyes," Neil explained, "but they do have brown dots where the eyes would be and a big mouth. When the grub matures, it digs through the top of the root and digs a tunnel to the surface. Then it sheds its skin and becomes a butterfly. The grub doesn't have to build a cocoon--its outer skin is its cocoon."

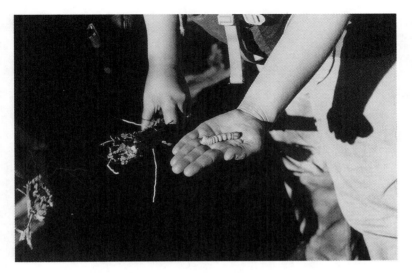

Michaela showing the witchity grub.

Neil shook the root vigorously until the witchity grub appeared. He pulled the grub out of its chamber and passed it around for everyone to feel. The three-inch-long, half-inch-diameter, ivory-colored grub was rubbery and covered with fine hairs. It was not slimy, dirty, smelly nor disgusting to look at. The head had a mouth with teeth. It digs with its mouth and can actually bite which was demonstrated as the grub supported its weight hanging from Neil's fingernail.

"The Aborigines throw the grubs in the fire and roast them or eat them raw," Neil said. "Personally, I like them raw. Anyone want to eat this one?"

Everyone backed away and shook their heads vigorously. Neil bit the head off the witchity grub while everyone in the group gagged and winced. Several people had enough composure to

Neil eating a witchity grub while a second one is coming out of the root.

take pictures as Neil dangled the grub from his mouth before chewing it up and swallowing it.

After his little show, he dug up the rest of the root and found another grub.

"So does anyone want to try one now?" Neil asked.

"Let Allen eat it," Michaela suggested. "He's the author and should have a first-hand experience so he can write about it."

This is one of the disadvantages of being a writer. People think you need these first-hand experiences--like falling off a cliff to write about how it feels just before you die. I knew I couldn't think about it very long or I would find a good reason not to do it. I grabbed the witchity grub from Neil, put it in my mouth, holding onto its head and bit down firmly. *Nothing happened.* The witchity grub has a very rubbery skin and I couldn't bite through it. Then I started to saw my teeth back and forth and pulled on the head until I finally cut through the skin.

As the head came off, I felt a soft, custard-like mass oozing out of the grub's body. No bones or anything else inside--just an oozy liquid. I chewed and swallowed the custard-like liquid. It had a very mild, neutral taste with a hint of almond flavor. There was no strong, bitter or objectionable taste. Actually it was almost tasteless except for the almond flavor--not bad at all. But I still had the skin in my mouth.

"It's like chewing gum," Neil said with a laugh.

And it was! I chewed and chewed and chewed. It took about five minutes before the skin finally disintegrated into small enough pieces to swallow. It definitely was an interesting experience. Would I do it again? Sure!

After I finished eating my grub, Michaela and Janice decided they wanted to try one. Neil dug around and found another. He cut it up so everyone could have a taste. *Bad move!* There were all kinds of brown and red and white things inside--the grubs vital organs. Once people saw the awful-looking mess, they wouldn't touch it.

We saw five more kangaroos as we rode along--one or two at a time. They sat near the trail until we rode close, then hopped up the side of the hills out of range and watched us pass, wary, but curious.

The bushes in the Australian Outback are inhospitable. Every bush seemed to reach out and grab me with its thorns or briars. When I walked, the briar inevitably worked its way down in my shoe and stuck my foot. Other briars tangled in my shoe laces and then stuck me as I tried to pull them out. Even when I rode, I seemed to get stuck by every tree we passed.

Camels are territorial animals like dogs or wolves. They mark their territory by rubbing their head on the bushes. Mick's scent gland was located between his ears on the back of his head.

The gland secreted a black, oily, smelly substance like creosote. As we passed a tree, Mick would rub his head on the branches to leave his mark, and smell the trees to see who else had been there.

Andrew pointed out some black "itchy grubs." They looked like a cute little black woolly worm--about an inch long and one-quarter-of-an-inch in diameter. Their fur is very prickly. The grub has a venom on its prickly fur that causes a terrible itch or rash if it crawls across your arm. Fortunately, no one played with the itchy grub or got "itched." We also saw centipedes.

"Those centipedes are more dangerous than the scorpions," Neil told us. "I've been bit by scorpions and got a little red spot that was sore for a day or two. But when a centipede walked across my foot, it left a sting that required medical attention."

I decided I needed a rear view mirror on my camel so I could keep track of the people behind. Whenever I was at the head of the group, I had to keep turning around to see if they were still behind or if everyone else had stopped to view some interesting sight. The way the saddle was built it was not easy to turn around. A rear view mirror would be a definite improvement.

The camels are extremely silent animals. They don't make any noise when they walk. They have huge soft peds on their feet and unless it is rutting season, they don't bellow, but just plod along silently. When we stopped for lunch and tied them to a tree, they sat quietly and rested--not a sound.

The neck muscle of a camel is fantastically strong. It supports a four-foot-long neck and a huge head. They are able to reach leaves or grass in about an eight-foot-diameter circle as they walk along the trail.

We passed some "silver dollar trees" or spinning gums. The leaves consist of two round (silver dollar sized) leaves

Lucy's camel, Bundi, was patient and well behaved as were all our camels.

attached to the stem. They look like helicopter blades. When I dropped them, they spun around like propellers.

Paul's camel, Comanche, had arthritis in its knees. It had a terrible time kneeling down. When Paul commanded him to kneel, Comanche would go down on its front legs and then stand there with its hind end up in the air and quiver. Paul would command him to kneel again and Comanche would start grunting and bellowing. It got so bad that Paul wouldn't even ask Comanche to kneel, but would just jump off while Comanche remained standing. Comanche was seven-feet high so it was quite a jump. When Paul wanted to get back up he would step on Comanche's knee, grab hold of the stirrup, jump up, grab the saddle horn, pull himself up with his strength and then wiggle into the saddle. All the other camels knelt on command, but not Comanche.

It was sunset when we started back to camp and dark by the time we arrived. Everyone gravitated to the blazing camp fire to warm up.

"The ABC television people were out here last year making a film on camels," Neil told us. "They hired several guys from the farm, including me, to do some camel riding for the film. In one scene they asked me to gallop down a rock-strewn hill on the camel hell-bent-for-leather. Well, I came riding down that death-defying hill, my camel jumping around the boulders, slipping and sliding on the rocks. When I got to the bottom, the ABC director called me over and said, 'Okay, now let's do it again'."

"Bull shit! I told him. You only get one try. I don't do these death-defying stunts over and over again," Neil said with a twinkle in his eye.

"How come you have that steel brace on your knee?" Tracy asked Andrew.

"Last year I was breaking some wild camels at the farm and one threw me off. I broke my leg when I fell. That healed in about six months so I could ride again without the brace. Then about three weeks ago I walked behind a young, wild camel and he kicked and knocked my knee out of joint. I don't wear this steel brace all the time, just when it starts hurting again."

"Do the camels tend to be mean?" I asked.

"They're vindictive," Andrew explained. "When a horse bucks, he just wants to throw you off. When a camel bucks, he wants to throw you off and stomp you. One time I got thrown by a wild camel and started climbing up the pen fence. That camel came after me when I was seven feet up the fence. He hit me with his front legs and knocked me off the fence. Then he tried to stomp me. I was lucky to get out of there alive. They're vindictive animals."

Before supper Mel took Paul and Nathan with him to collect firewood. Mel drove the truck with the trailer hooked up and they picked up pieces of firewood when they came across them. Mel wouldn't let the boys pick up one dead tree because it had a snake hole in the side of it and he was afraid the snake might still be in the tree.

"Snakes don't burn too well," Mel related when he returned.

Shortly after Mel arrived back with the firewood, he rang the dinner bell. We feasted on plump chicken breasts in oriental sauce with pineapple slices over a steaming plate of white rice and mixed vegetables. We ate a variety of tasty foods on this safari. Even the kids cleaned their plates and went back for seconds.

After supper I decided to take a hot shower. The camp had a 20-gallon water tank with a firebox under it. I loaded the firebox with kindling, lit it and waited 20 minutes for the water to heat. The shower was in a little shed with no door. When I got in the shower, the water was good and hot--I stood there soaking for five minutes, washed and rinsed off. The air temperature was about 40F when I stepped out. Needless to say, it didn't take me long to dry off, get my clothes on and get back by the fire. Kelsey, Tracy and Paul took their showers in the morning when it was even colder.

"Dennis Wickham, the famous Australian naturalist, is back at the camel farm tonight," Andrew said as we sat around the fire. "He's leaving to take a camel ride across the Simpson Desert next Tuesday. Dennis has walked across the desert and driven a gypsy caravan pulled by a camel across the desert."

"I met him on one of his trips when I was driving my Subaru across the Simpson," Lilly recalled. "He invited me over for a cuppa. Dennis told me he had lost his favorite chair. I mentioned that I'd seen a chair in the middle of the road about 10 miles back. There was an empty bottle of Bundy rum sitting beside it. Dennis nodded sadly and said, 'Yes, that's where I got drunk last night'."

Janice related her experiences on a trip to India where she and Lucy visited the Taj Mahal.

"We saw it by moonlight. It was fantastic!"

Kate, a new member of our group who had joined us for the middle three days of the trip, related her trips around Australia. The subject of the supernatural came up and Mel asked if I'd ever traveled through the Bermuda Triangle?

"Yeah," I replied. "In 1976 we were flying our Air Force Boeing-707 test aircraft through the Bermuda Triangle one dark night when something sucked the plane out of the sky. One minute we were okay and the next minute the plane was diving straight for the water at a speed approaching Mach One. Miraculously, the pilot was able to pull the plane up just before we hit the water. They did a month of testing on the airplane after that and were never able to figure out what got us in that mess in the first place."

Annette brought up the subject of aliens. *Everyone* had something to add to that topic. Then Andrew started telling Australian jokes. Almost all the Australian jokes illustrated the chauvinistic attitude of the Australian men towards women, like when Crocodile Dundee told his female companion in the movie she couldn't survive in the wild because she was just a sheila. Andrew also liked to tell New Zealand jokes (similar to our Polish or redneck jokes).

"A New Zealander invented the toilet seat in 1852. One year later, an Australian improved the invention by cutting a hole in it," Andrew joked.

Annette and Lucy offered to get coffee and tea for us as we sat around the fire. When they returned with the drinks, they had put Weet-Bix cereal in Andrew's and Neil's coffee. Later, Mel brought out an apple cake and passed pieces around. He had put pepper on top of Annette's. One of Lucy's boots disappeared during the evening. Andrew insisted the dingoes (wild Australian dogs) had sneaked in the camp and run off with it. The next morning we found Lucy's boot at the edge of the camp where the dingo apparently dropped it.

"I'm tired," admitted Lilly, "but I hate to go to bed while everyone else is up because I'm afraid I'll miss something." Everyone agreed. We usually sat around the campfire telling stories until midnight. Tracy and Kelsey went to bed about 10 o'clock, but Paul would stay up with the rest of us. He just sat there and listened for three or four hours without saying a word. If someone asked him a direct question, he'd answer with a simple yes or no. He never asked questions or entered into the conversation, just listened.

We were riding 15 or 20 miles every day. During the breaks we did a lot of walking while exploring the canyons and

71

Annette, Janice, Michaela and Lucy thinking up tricks to play on Andrew.

caves. By the time we arrived back at camp I was tired, but not exhausted. I went to bed between 11 o'clock and midnight and woke up completely rested at 4 or 5 a.m.

Several times during the night I woke and looked up at the beautiful night sky. There was a different pattern in the sky every time I looked up. Quite often I saw a meteor shoot across the sky--part of the August meteor shower. Early in the morning, an hour before sunrise, I could see satellites go across the sky. Ninety miles north of our camp, at Alice Springs, there is a satellite tracking station called Pine Gap. They read out the information from the low-altitude spy satellites. These satellites are programmed to go directly over Alice Springs so they can dump the data. The satellites looked like stars, but they moved very rapidly--crossing the sky in five or ten minutes.

CHAPTER 7

THE FIRST AUSTRALIANS

Primitive, stone-age, savage--words often applied to the original Australians, the Aborigines. In Alice Springs and Ayers Rock I had the opportunity to talk to many of them, but we never encountered any in the desert on our camel safari. When the Europeans came to Australia in the 1600s and 1700s, they labeled the Aborigines "primitive," Stone-Age throwbacks, savages. They didn't fit the "Bell Curve" as described by Herrnstein & Murray, 1994.

The original inhabitants of Australia migrated from South-East Asia and Indonesia during the last great Ice Age, 50,000 to 80,000 years ago. It wasn't a single migration by a single blood line, but a series of migrations over tens of thousands of years. By the time the first Europeans arrived in Australia, it is estimated there were 300,000 to 500,000 Aborigines living in about 500 kinship or territorial tribal groups. Today, there are 50,000 to 100,000 Aborigines who survived disease and extermination which accompanied the arrival of the Europeans. One of the early European settlers noted, "It will be a happy day for Australia when the natives and kangaroos disappear. The time has come for drastic, exact and positive measures, administered not with a light hand," (Hasluck, 1942). The drastic action was the extermination of several hundred thousand Aborigines.

Before the Europeans arrived, a typical Aboriginal camp consisted of 10 to 50 people. They were semi-nomadic, traveling in a fairly small geographic area, moving as the game became scarce or fruit and berries ripened around an established circuit. The original inhabitants relied on nature to provide their daily needs. They had no domesticated animals and did no farming. Their most striking traits that proved them primitive, as far as the Europeans were concerned, was they had *no written language and no material possessions.*

Captain James Cook sailed around Australia in 1770 and noted in his diary: "The Aborigines have no need for our gifts. We offered them clothes, beads, trinkets, tinware, shoes, blankets and food. They seemed to set no value upon anything we gave them nor would they ever part with anything of theirs for one article we could offer!" (Whitlock & Carter, 1992).

The Aborigines wore no clothes, had no iron implements, no jewelry, no written language, no currency, no permanent cooking utensils, no permanent shelter. When they moved, they carried a hunting club, a spear and a small "dilly" bag with their sacred shells, feathers and bones. Nature provided for their needs when they arrived at a new camp. This was not in the Garden of Eden. It was in the driest part of the driest continent in the world where every bush and plant was full of burrs and stickers. Wherever they roamed, they encountered more poisonous insects, spiders and snakes than nonpoisonous ones. In this hostile environment, the Aborigines became so attuned to nature that they found water where there appeared to be none; tracked game over solids rocks; identified hundreds of edible roots, seeds and fruit; and located where insects stored their honey for nourishment.

The Aborigines developed a religion based on nature with a definite set of rules, taboos and rites that governed their lives. For example, if a man saw his mother-in-law coming down the path toward him, he was required to step off the path and let her pass without speaking to her.   That rule apparently helped to avoid a lot of arguments.

They did not see themselves as unique or superior to nature's other animals, but as an integral part of nature. There was no "chief" in an Aboriginal camp or tribal group. A group of elders made the decisions, enforced the laws and settled disputes. They had a well-understood set of moral codes by which to live and punished those who broke the codes.   It is interesting that during their 50,000 years in Australia, the Aborigines *never* found the need for a formalized war against their neighboring tribes. They didn't raid neighboring tribes to kidnap "slaves" as the civilized Europeans did to the Aborigines in the 1800s. The Aborigines didn't massacre their neighbors to steal their land or possessions as the Europeans did to them. They didn't slaughter their neighbors because of different religious beliefs as the rest of the civilized world has done and continues to do.

If an Aborigine from one tribe had a complaint against a person from another tribe, they didn't go to war to settle the dispute. The tribes gathered and watched as the two individuals involved in the dispute threw spears at each other or fought in hand-to-hand combat.   Once the pair settled their dispute, whatever the outcome, the tribes went peacefully on their separate ways.

"The Aborigines are not survivors of a Stone-Age culture. They are our contemporaries, modern men and women, motivated by the same basic urges as ourselves, but traditionally with a different way of life, different outlook and different values. And differences need not imply inequality." (Berndt, 1964).

The Aborigines believed the primordial land was given to them by mythical beings in Dream Time. These mythical beings shaped the land and humanized it. While they have many sacred sites where specific events took place, the Aborigines believed "the whole land is sacred!"   They lived like Greenpeace advocates.   In their 50,000 years of occupation, the Aborigines didn't "change" any of Australia.   The changes to nature in Australia took place only after the Europeans arrived.

Old age brought rewards and security in the Aboriginal society.   The elderly were viewed with more leniency, surrounded by less stress and experienced less loneliness than in European society.

The Aborigines were often viewed as primitive because they lacked a written language.   In a society such as theirs without a written language, initiation, rituals and rites were the core of their social and cultural life.   Only through the indoctrination of the young could traditional customs and beliefs be maintained.   Knowledge had to be transmitted through systematic rites to keep the traditions alive.

Tradition has it that in the beginning, the Aboriginal women possessed all the knowledge.   The women soon realized this was not right, so according to the women, they *gave* part of the knowledge to the men.   The men's version is that they *stole* the knowledge from the women.   Labor was shared--men hunted, women gathered.   These chores only required a few hours a day, which left plenty of time for the more pleasant pursuits such as storytelling, gossiping, singing, dancing and social contact.

The Aborigines had native "doctors" who cured illness with special medicinal herbs, salves of crushed grubs or magic potions.   They possessed a strong knowledge of *magic* and *folk* cures handed down generation to generation.   The healing power of faith has been proven in all cultures including our sophisticated ones.   The native doctors used *magic* or faith to remove curses or misfortunes that were troubling their patients.   To differentiate themselves from the non-practitioners, the doctors often cut off the tip of their index finger.   Many cave drawings depict the hand of an Aboriginal doctor with the index fingertip missing.   This mutilation added to the aura of their mystical powers.

The Aborigines understood the relationship of intercourse and pregnancy. However, they didn't believe that intercourse was the only ingredient in the development of life. They believed that the soul or spiritual aspects of life required a "spirit child" to attach itself to the fetus before it was born. The pregnant woman obtained the spirit child when she visited a sacred site, from some natural feature of the land or from some animal or bird. When the identity of the spirit child was determined, it became a special and personal totem for the baby.

The Aboriginal social order consisted of a well understood set of taboos and a system for enforcing them. When someone had a complaint against another person, he could bring the alleged *crime* to the attention of the elders of a tribe. They called a council and investigate the evidence. Once a verdict was reached, the punishment was decided. Punishment could have been a public scolding or payment of some small gift for minor infractions, banishment from the camp or tribe for more serious crimes or death for the most serious transgressions. A tribal policeman, the Kurdatcha Man, was contacted to carry out the sentence (Keneally, 1983). The Kurdatcha Man's identity was known only to a few elders in the tribe. When he carried out a sentence, he dressed in an emu-feather costume, complete with an emu-feather helmet and emu-feather boots. He could kill a convicted person by "pointing the bone" at him. It was a magical bone made from the thigh-bone of a kangaroo or human. After it was pointed at him, the convicted person simply went off and died. Australian (European) doctors tried to intervene in some cases and "save" the victim, but as soon as he was out of the care of the doctor, he died anyway. In some cases the Kurdatcha Man meted out the punishment in a more physical manner, such as hurling a spear in the back, throwing the convicted off a cliff or setting him on fire. This practice continues today in Australia, but to a lesser extent. The Australian justice system has tried to prosecute suspected Kurdatcha Men following a suspicious death, but they have never been able to find anyone who was willing to testify against the tribal executioner.

Evaluating a culture solely in terms of what the people did to provide for their livelihood or survival provides only a limited perspective. As Berndt, 1964, noted, "What people do outside of the sphere of necessity is especially significant! The great mythic epics and song cycles of the Aborigines demonstrated beyond doubt a high level of cultural attainment. They established a very original and unique form of painting, art and sculpture. Anyone conversing with fully-initiated Aborigines trained in the sacred myths and songs cannot fail to be aware that he is in the presence of men of education and culture."

The enduring characteristics of the Australian Aboriginal society are:

> *Affinity with the land,*
> *Harmony with nature,*
> *Cooperativeness,*
> *Love of beauty,*
> *Aesthetic appreciation,*
> *Respect for the past,*
> *Recognition of personal rights and responsibilities,*
> *Low state of aggressiveness,*
> *Adherence to a positive, nonviolent religion.*

If these are the characteristics of a primitive, savage society, we need to rethink the desirability of our sophisticated, civilized one.

CHAPTER 8

THE CRICKET PITCH

A tiny sliver of the moon popped up as I was getting dressed about an hour before sunrise. I threw a couple of logs on the fire, stirred it up and walked over to check on Tracy and Kelsey. A small hank of blonde hair stuck out from one side of the sleeping bag and a clump of brunette hair from the other. Tracy and Kelsey both slept with their noses under the covers which was the logical thing to do when you're sleeping outdoors in freezing temperatures.

I built a fire under the hot-water tank and heated the shower water before I woke the kids. Once the water was hot, I reached under the sleeping bag and grabbed Kelsey's foot.

"Grandpa!" she yelled. "Don't!"

Slowly I extracted Kelsey feet-first from under the sleeping bag.

"Grandpa, it's cold!"

"Put your coat and shoes on and come over to take your shower."

"Let Tracy take her shower first," Kelsey yelled as she pulled the covers around her.

"No, Tracy took her shower first last time. Today you're first."

Reluctantly, Kelsey put her coat on over her nightgown, slid into her shoes and ran for the shower building. I adjusted the water to the right temperature before she jumped in. While Kelsey was showering, I went back to her hut, selected some clean clothes for her and brought them back to the shower room. After five minutes, I had to pry Kelsey out of the warm water into the cold morning air.

"Dry off quick and get into your clothes," I told her. Then I woke Tracy and she showered.

After breakfast I walked over to check on Mick while I was still eating a piece of toast. Mick watched me intensely with his big brown eyes and begged for a bite of toast.

"No toast, Mick. It's not on the approved diet for camels," I said as I walked around behind him. He turned his head to follow my every move, never taking his eyes off the toast. Finally he shamed me sufficiently so I offered it to him. He reached with his huge lips pursed out beyond his teeth and deftly grabbed it from my hand. As he chewed it he had a look of complete satisfaction on his face as if to say, "Thank you!"

The previous night Neil noticed that Jeda and Moses had cuts on their feet. This morning Kelsey joined me at the pen and asked how Jeda's foot was.

"Looks pretty bad," I said, and pointed to Jeda who was favoring her left-front foot.

"Will Tracy be able to ride her this morning?" Kelsey asked.

"I don't think she'll be able to walk on it today," I said, "but Jeda has three good feet to walk on. We can fix her up with a crutch for that bad leg."

"Grandpa, is that true?" Kelsey asked as she eyed me with suspicion. She turned to Lucy and asked, "Is that true, Lucy?"

"Yes," Lucy supported my story, "camels can walk with a crutch."

Neil came up about that time so Kelsey asked him, also.

"Oh, yeah," Neil said with a twinkle in his eye. "I keep a pair of camel crutches out in the saddle-shed. I'll just strap a crutch on Jeda and she'll be fine."

Kelsey didn't seem convinced. Neil put some more salve on Jeda's foot, but she was still limping on that left-front foot, almost stumbling. Neil walked her around a bit and decided the foot would be okay.

When we headed out on the trail, Tracy commanded Jeda to kneel, mounted and commanded her to get up. She then walked Jeda around the pen. At first Jeda limped and held her foot up periodically, but after a few minutes she was walking normally on it. We started our ride. An hour later Jeda showed no sign of a limp. Later in the day she was running and never did favor that foot again. Apparently she didn't want to wear that clumsy camel crutch.

Following the trail we came to a range fence, turned and rode alongside it.

"Does the fence keep the wild camels in as well as the cows?" I asked Neil who was riding alongside me.

"No. A camel can get under a fence through a very small opening," he replied. "They actually lay down and roll underneath, something a cow can't do. Camels are very smart and can crawl underneath a stock fence if the bottom wire isn't low enough."

As we rode along single file, Paul and his camel, Comanche, galloped past and pulled back in front of me. Mick stretched out his long neck and bit Comanche on the butt to let him know he was in the wrong place. For the rest of the day I could still see the red teeth marks on Comanche's rear.

Mick was taking about a five-foot pace as we walked along the flat trail. His normal gait was about one step per second. If you did the math, which I did to pass the time, that worked out to a rate of between three and four miles per hour.

The kids became bored as we rode along and started a game where they picked seeds, about the size of olive pits, off the trees we passed. The four of them ran a contest to see who could pick the most seeds. Kelsey soon had both pockets full; Paul was more resourceful--he borrowed a plastic bag and soon had it full. Tracy and Nathan filled their hats. After a while they tired of the picking game and started a seed-throwing game. They would gallop past and fling seeds at each other. That was okay until they decided to gang up and throw seeds at the adults. The game was soon stopped.

I have not seen any true cactus in the Australian desert similar to the ones we have in our American deserts. They have all kinds of sticky, spiny things, but no succulent cactus like our sequaro, barrel or organ-pipe cactus.

The temperature rose a little higher each day. Usually it was noon before I stripped down to my T-shirt. This day, I was sweating before we stopped for our morning tea at 10:30. The temperature approached 100 degrees with no breeze as we rode through the valleys. Andrew hurried us along, saying we could see the train go by if we rode a little faster.

"Woooooo, woooooo," I heard the train's sorrowful whistle as we rode through a long, stony gorge. We missed the only train of the day.

About noon we exited the gorge and rode out onto a flat plain near the Ghan Railroad. Just ahead of us was a dry lake with a cricket pitch in the center. Andrew explained that 20 years ago when a British company was laying a new section of track nearby for the Ghan Railroad, the British workers built a cricket pitch here. Rain doesn't fall very often in this desert. The cricket pitch was still there, still usable. The old Ghan Railroad was built by an Afghan crew 100 years ago from Adelaide up to Alice

Neil made a fire for our morning billy-tea break.

Springs. The new line takes a slightly different route a mile or two to the east of the old line.

The spot Neil picked for lunch was on a rocky ledge 50 feet above the desert floor. It was under the north-facing wall which was shady and cool. While the desert sun was blistering hot, there was a cool breeze in the shade and a jacket felt good. Andrew produced lunch from his saddle-bags. Spam, corned beef, potatoes, corn, asparagus, peas, bread and a delicious fruit cake for dessert. Neil built the fire with the wood that Janice gathered and put the billy on to boil. When the water was hot, Tracy put the tea in and poured after the tea steeped.

I tied Mick up to a spiny tree before lunch. It looked like a Christmas tree, but had very prickly needles. When I reached in to tie the reins to a branch, the needles stuck me. My hand was

Mick usually napped during our tea break.

covered with hundreds of prickly spines. While I ate my lunch, Mick ate the prickly tree branches. He had a real tough mouth.

The trail became very dusty as the wind picked up after lunch. The sandy soil was being swept up and thrown in our faces. We came to a 30-foot-high hill of smooth, solid rock. I was a little concerned about how the camels were going to keep their footing on the steep solid rock, but Mick just trudged up the rock hill without a problem. His large, soft peds gripped the rock as he silently plodded up the incline.

Andrew had a little trouble with his camel, Thumper, who was half wild and still being broken. When he tried to hurry Thumper up the hill, Thumper opened his mouth like a jackass and bellowed loudly. His short tail stood straight out as he reluctantly climbed and continued to bellow.

This day's ride turned out to be our longest. There were no sacred caves to explore, no water holes nor fossil beds to dig in. We just rode and rode and rode--eight hours in the saddle. Just two quick comfort stops and a short lunch break--a marathon ride.

After supper Michaela entertained us with stories of her past.

"I was born in Austria in the 60s and raised in Vienna. At 20 years of age, I started on my first adventure--a 7,000 kilometer drive across the Sahara Desert. We drove in an Austrian military car, a Pinzgauer made by the company Steyr Daimler Puch. It was a great four-wheel-drive vehicle. Our route followed the old French military tracks, navigating with maps and a compass. The desert was intimidating as we drove for days across the endless sand dunes without encountering a soul! We took enough drinking water, petrol and food for 10 days. At each oasis we filled our car with petrol, refilled our water tanks, took a long shower and continued our journey.

"After that adventure I developed a passion for deserts. The absolute silence was fascinating. It was an escape from all the city noises. The clear skies at night and the crisp mornings were lovely. The most beautiful sights were the sand dunes in the late afternoon or early morning. It's interesting how things survive in such a fragile environment.

"Since that first trip, I've traveled on all continents. I came to Alice Springs two years ago to see Ayers Rock and the Olgas. That trip inspired me to learn more about the Australian desert. Seeing it from the back of a camel seemed an appropriate way to do it.

"I emigrated to Australia last year and work in desktop publishing. My other hobbies are cooking and watching foreign films and documentaries. I also collect music from all parts of the world," Michaela concluded.

85

After Michaela's story, Andrew treated us to an Australian joke.

These two mates had been carrying their swag together through the Outback for years. Early one morning while following a parched creek bed, they passed the body of a large animal, black and bloated. About midday Bill took the pipe out of his mouth and grunted, "D'yer see the dead ox?" There was no reply from his mate. The shadows of evening were closing around them when Jim spat softly and said, "T'weren't no ox. T'was a 'orse." Shortly later, Jim turned in and got a good night's sleep. When he awoke the next morning, there was no sign of Bill or Bill's swag--just a grimy note scrawled and tucked in a cleft stick. "There's too much arguing in this here camp," it said.

"That reminds me of the one about the swagman who was tramping along an Outback road through the big sheep paddocks," Mel chimed in.

Each paddock had a gate which had to be opened by anyone going through and closed after him so the sheep wouldn't get out. The plain extends endlessly in all directions. A heat haze simmers on the horizon--not a building or tree in sight. Along came a grazier driving a big Cadillac. He stopped beside the swagman. "Hop in," he says. "I'll give you a lift."

"No thanks," replies the swagman, trudging on.

The grazier scratched his head over the response. "Wonder what's wrong with the fellow." Then he let out the clutch and drove slowly abreast of the swagman again. "C'mon! Hop in and I'll give you a lift." The swagman silently shook his head and kept walking. The grazier sat for a few minutes. By now he was completely perplexed. He drove up again, stopped in front of the swagman, and opened the passenger door.

"Come on," he says. "Don't be a bloody fool. Hop in and I'll give you a lift."

"No thanks, Mate," he says grimly. "You can open your own bloody gates!"

(Mel had to explain the joke to me. It was the passenger's responsibility to hop out of the car every 15 or 20 minutes to open and shut the paddock gates so the car could pass through.)

CHAPTER 9

THE SYMPHONY

The scene in the pen was straight out of the Arabian Nights--Neil leading 11 camels single file in the dawn's half-light. The nose line of each camel was tied to the tail of the camel in front. He led Mick, the dominant bull, and all the other camels followed passively behind.

The morning started out warm and windy with the promise of a hot day. We passed a stand of beechwood trees and I saw a flock of blue-green parrots sitting on the branches.

"Squawk, squawk, squawk," they complained as we interrupted their socializing.

One of the tree branches contained a tubular nest about three inches in diameter and a foot long.

"That's an itchy-grub nest," Neil said. "The caterpillar pricks your skin with its sharp hairs. If you scratch them, it actually drives the needle-like hairs further in your skin. I've seen people scratch until they bled. Best thing is just to wash the area and leave it alone."

Andrew led us along the Hugh River, a dry, sandy riverbed about 50-feet wide. He told us that during the Spring rains, the river depth could reach 20-feet. We saw testimony to the high water--huge pieces of driftwood up in the tops of some of the ghost gum trees along the bank.

Neil heard the emus beating their wings as a danger signal.

As we crossed a sandy hill, Neil put his hand up, signaling us to stop.

"Hear that?" Neil asked.

I listened intently, but all I could hear was the wind in the trees.

"It's an emu drumming," Neil whispered. "The female is beating her wings to warn the others that there's danger in the area. They travel in male-female pairs. It sounds like there are several pairs over the hill. Let me see if I can turn them and get them to come back this way," he said as he got off his camel and sneaked through the bush. We could hear him making an emu call and the birds replying, but the sounds got further and further away. About 10 minutes later Neil returned.

"They just kept going," he shrugged.

We stopped for lunch along the riverbed. As I sat down, a huge shadow swept over me. I looked up and saw a wedge-tailed eagle directly overhead. The eight-foot-wing-span eagle soared back and forth across the riverbed looking for something or somebody to eat. Andrew said they could carry off a small kangaroo.

Neil pointed out the ants scurrying around the site, particularly active. "That usually means rain. The ants build up a little dike around their hole to keep the rain out. The Aborigines could read the ant's activity and predict the weather."

We ate lunch and then walked down the riverbed to a beautiful white-sand beach. Janice decided to lay down to sun bathe.

"Let's bury Janice in the sand," Lucy joked.

"Okay," Janice agreed.

The four kids thought that was great fun so they piled sand on top of her until only her head was showing. Someone tied two sticks together to form a little cross and stuck it at the end near her head. Several of us photographed our first casualty of the camel trek.

"What are these tracks?" Kelsey asked Neil, pointing to some big tracks in the sand.

"Those are goanna tracks," Neil replied.

"What's a goanna?" was her next question.

"The goanna is a fierce lizard that grows to be three- or four-feet long. Its jaws are so powerful it can bite right through your hand. And it has tremendously sharp claws. I saw one bloke try to grab a big goanna once. The goanna bit the fellow's hand and held on. When he finally managed to get his hand out of its mouth, the goanna clawed the bloke's other arm. The guy was a bloody mess. I used to raise goannas in Sydney for the wildlife park. The way I caught them was to grab the tail. Then I'd lift their back feet off the ground and walk them around like a wheel

During our tea break we buried Janice in the sand.

barrow with only their front feet on the ground. They couldn't turn around or do anything that way."

"Is that true?" Kelsey asked skeptically.

"Absolutely true," Neil replied. "I gave up camel handling about seven years ago, moved to Sydney, got married and we had a baby girl. She's six-years old now. I made my living raising and handling snakes and lizards for a wildlife park. I used to keep brown snakes, red-bellied snakes and goannas in our house. My wife didn't like that too much and finally divorced me. I just moved back to the camel farm a couple of weeks ago."

As I got back in the saddle, Mick stretched his head back to my foot. I thought he was going to bite me, but he just scratched his soft nose on the toe of my boot to relieve an itch. His neck was amazingly flexible, reaching all the way back to his side.

We followed along the high bank of the river. Every 100 yards or so we would cross another little ravine that ran into the river. Our trail was up and down, up and down, up and down the ravines. Each seemed to be a little bit deeper than the last. Eventually we were riding up and down 30-foot-deep ravines. It was pretty exciting on a camel.

The trees along the river were primarily of the gum variety, but we also encountered corkwood, ironwood, acacia and beechwood trees. We stopped by a huge tree with a trunk about 10 feet across.

"They say this is the largest ghost gum in Australia," Andrew told us.

"Why is it called a ghost gum tree?" Kelsey asked.

"Because it's so white. On a moonless night when you can't see anything else, the ghost gums stand out in the dark."

As we started riding again I marveled at how perceptive Mick was. He responded instantly to my request to turn. I would think about turning left and he turned left, think about turning right and he turned right. Obviously, I must have made some small motion with the reins or my knees, but Mick was very perceptive of where I wanted to go.

I had brought an orange from the camp for a snack. Mid-afternoon Kelsey asked me to peel it for her. As I started peeling the orange, Mick looked over his shoulder and decided he would like to have a bite of it. He reached around and tried to take the orange away from me while I was still peeling it. I told him it was for Kelsey. When I finished I held a piece of the rind out to the side. Mick turned around, stuck his lips out six inches beyond his teeth and delicately picked it from my hand. He seemed to enjoy it so much that I decided to give him a quarter of the orange along with the peelings. I rode up next to Kelsey and handed her the rest of the orange.

The temperature climbed to 100F by mid-afternoon. I was hot and tired. On the ride back to camp, I started visualizing a nice shower to wash the sweat and dust off me. As soon as we arrived back, I fired up the hot-water tank and set out my clean clothes. A few minutes later I was standing in the hot shower soaking away the aches and pains of the day. It's amazing how a hot shower can improve one's outlook.

After supper, Andrew offered to drive us over to Rainbow Valley to witness the brilliant colors of a desert sunset on the sandstone cliffs. We didn't take the camels because they don't have headlights. It would be dark before we returned. The 10 of us and Andrew piled into the truck and headed for Rainbow Valley. It had been a hard week on the trail. I knew I was getting physically tired, but I hadn't anticipated hallucinations. As we approached the large, dry lake clay-pan that stretched a mile in front of the Rainbow Valley cliffs, I imagined I heard classical music coming from beyond the hill.

"It's just the wind whistling through the tree tops," Michaela suggested.

The colors of the Rainbow Valley hills were magnificent at sunset.

"Yeah, but it has perfect pitch," I noted.

As the dry lake came into view, we found ourselves face-to-face with a complete symphony orchestra! Twenty violins, oboes, cellos, a kettle drum, base fiddles, brass and a grand piano. Seated in concentric rows were the 100 members of a symphony orchestra--dressed in formal black attire!

I closed my eyes and shook my head. When I opened them, the orchestra reappeared playing "I Still Call Australia Home." In addition, there were three or four ground camera units and an aerial camera operator in a cherry picker.

"We're filming a Qantas Airlines commercial," the on-site director explained. "We've been all around the world shooting scenes: Amsterdam, Los Angeles, Beijing and London. This is the closing scene for the commercial."

We watched a magnificent, golden desert sunset make the Rainbow Valley sandstone cliffs glow in fiery reds, vibrant pinks, subtle beiges and brilliant whites as the cameras captured the images and sound. The orchestra continued to play as the sun sank lower in the sky and the colors grew more vibrant. I can't imagine a more impressive setting for a symphony concert. It captured all the emotions of our fantastic week of exploring the Red Center on camels--amazement, fear, excitement, discovery, pain and pleasure.

The director told us they had been there all day and had shot about 30,000 feet of film. The commercial's edited clip would be about three feet of film--a five-second clip for the closing scene.

When we got back to camp we sat around the fire and told stories. The subject of dingoes came up.

"Do they cause much trouble?" I asked.

"Around here it's mostly cattle country. Dingoes aren't much of a problem," Neil explained. "But south of the dog fence in sheep country, they can really raise hell. Dingoes love to kill lambs--not necessarily to eat them, just kill them for the sport of it. I heard tell of a pack of dingoes killing 40 or 50 lambs in one night. Now when that happens, the sheep ranchers will offer a big reward for dead dingoes.

"Couple of years ago a mate of mine and I went down to South Australia to make some bounty money. Seemed a pack of dingoes was causing a terrible ruckus there. We built ourselves a big fire near one of the sheering pens where a bunch of sheep and lambs were being kept. In the middle of the night, the dingoes would try to sneak in and get to the lambs. My mate and I would wait until we could see the reflection of the fire in their eyes and then shot between their eyes. We got two dingoes the first night before the others were scared off.

95

"Now them dingoes are pretty sly fellows. The second night I must have shot at five or six and never hit one. Figured my sights must have gotten bumped or something. So next day I re-sighted my rifle and found it was dead on.

"That night when the eyes of the first dingo appeared in the firelight I switched on my five-cell torch and got the shock of my life. Instead of one dingo, there were two dingoes. They were standing about four or five inches apart. One dingo had his left eye closed and the other had his right eye closed. I was shooting right between them darn dingoes!" Neil concluded with a grin.

Earlier Mel had mixed up some damper, an unleavened bread, poured it in a cast-iron pan with a lid and buried it in the hot coals of the fire. When Neil finished his story, Mel dug the pan out of the coals and served the hot bread with melted butter, jam and tea. The smell of fresh bread piqued everybody's appetite. Delicious!

As we ate our damper, Lilly told us a little about her life. She was born in Zurich, Switzerland and after high school studied retailing and commercial trades. At age 21 she was in charge of a floor in a large department store.

"Life was very pleasant in those days," Lilly continued. "I had many friends and interests: walking, dancing or just sitting at an outdoor cafe with friends philosophizing about the meaning of life. At age 22 I married and 5 months later my husband and I emigrated to Australia. It was a disastrous marriage. My husband kept me in virtual isolation--no friends or family to confide in. At the time I didn't understand what was happening, but later I realized my husband had mental problems. He desperately wanted to be a martyr for his faith and needed a persecutor. Unbeknownst to me, he allocated that role to me after he failed to convert me to his extreme beliefs. For him, all went well. He could make me cringe, crawl, cry and always comply. After 25 years of that hell I left him, taking our eight-year-old son with me. It was very difficult because I had forgotten how to interact or even converse with normal people. In an effort to regain my confidence I began driving through the Outback. There, I could relax and found I could talk to anyone I met without getting tongue-tied.

"Now I live on a farm in New South Wales and raise a few black sheep. Black wool used to be the rage, but I don't sell the wool any more. I spin a little for myself and knit," Lilly concluded.

I'm amazed at how adventurous these Australian women are. Lilly drove 400 miles across the Simpson desert by herself; Lucy went off on an 18-month backpack trip through Indonesia, Thailand, Nepal, India, Sri-Lanka, Egypt, Jordan, Syria, Israel, Turkey, Italy and Switzerland. Michaela drove an army truck across the trackless Sahara desert. Even my travel agent, Jodi, took a two-year working vacation in Europe and spent eight weeks in South Africa. She was chased by a hippo on a lake in Zimbabwe, white-water rafted at Victoria Falls and had a roaring lion walk into her tent-camp in Botswana. The average American college student thinks traveling around the Continent on a Euro-Rail Pass is a big adventure.

CHAPTER 10

THE LONG RIDE HOME

Dingo Attack!!!

When Annette got up in the morning she discovered that one of her boots that she had set alongside her sleeping bag was missing. Andrew swore he saw dingo tracks around the camp and speculated that a dingo stole the boot. A thorough search by our entire camp turned up the missing boot in Nathan's bed.

"See the teeth marks," Andrew said as he returned the boot to Annette. Annette interpreted the scuff marks on the side of the boot as just that--scuff marks or maybe Nathan's teeth marks.

Everyone seemed a little melancholy this morning because our adventure was coming to a close. Even the camels were restless during the night. Neil had to break up a fight between several of them. Apparently they understood it was time to go back to the farm and were testing Mick's dominance. Fortunately, none of the camels were hurt.

This was our last morning. It was time to strip our swag and stuff all the sheets in the pillowcase. Then we rolled up the swag and tied a strap around it. As I went through the motions I felt like it was the day after Christmas and all the surprises were over for another year.

For breakfast we had bum nuts from a chuck and a cuppa. Translation: eggs from a chicken and a cup of tea.

After breakfast, we packed our bags and put them in the back of the truck. I climbed up on Mick and was sitting there thinking about all that had happened the past seven days.

"Grandpa, you and Mick look the same," Kelsey said. *"Old and grumpy."*

Out of the mouth of babes comes the truth! I felt old and grumpy.

At first light we started our ride back to Noel Fullerton's camel farm. We rode through a stand of corkwood trees, and Neil pointed out some big bird nests and a number of birds the size of magpies sitting in the trees.

"Those are Apostle birds sometimes called white-browed babbler," Neil explained. "Twelve birds live in a single nest. It's an extended family with the elder birds, the adults, adolescents and babies all in one nest. The birds help one another and feed each other's young."

As we rode by I could hear them singing. Their song consisted of five repetitions of a single note.

"Tweet-tweet-tweet-tweet-tweet."

"Look at the big eggs!" Kelsey shouted as she pointed to a half-dozen egg-shaped, green objects laying in the sand.

"Those are paddy melons," Neil explained. "The Aborigines drink the liquid for nourishment and use the outer rind as bowls." The paddy melons, which were the size of an ostrich egg, grew on a thin, leafless vine. Once Kelsey mentioned them, I looked around and saw one vine that had grown up into a bush. The melons hung off the bush like giant green apples.

When we stopped by a water hole for lunch, Tracy called our attention to all the birds in the nearby trees. There were zebra finches with their distinctive red beaks, half-a-dozen iridescent blue-winged rosella parakeets and numerous other colorful birds.

Lilly pointed out a giant iridescent blue moth resting on a bush by the water. Two wedge-tail eagles were circling high

Kelsey found some paddy melons that looked like giant eggs.

overhead. Life flourished around the water hole this morning.

      Kate had returned to the farm mid-week so Paul rode Kate's camel to give Comanche's arthritis a rest. After lunch, Andrew was leading Comanche behind his camel when something spooked him. He reared up, pulled his nose plug out and took off wild-eyed for the hills spewing blood from his nose. Neil got down from his camel, Fruba, and started running after Comanche. I'm not sure why he didn't ride after him, but his strategy worked and Neil caught Comanche a few minutes later. Andrew brought Comanche's reins over to Neil with the nose plug still attached. Neil washed the nose plug, sponged the blood off Comanche's nose with cool water and poked the nose plug back into place. Comanche didn't move as Neil talked and worked with him. Then he handed the reins back to Andrew and there were no further problems with Comanche.

We rode through a gully and passed a number of ant hills a foot in diameter and four inches high. Instead of having a round opening for the ant hole, there was a two-inch long, quarter inch wide slit.

"Those are bull-dog ant holes," Andrew told us, "the ants with the big pinchers."

Periodically Mick took a deep breath and held it. His chest swelled up another foot in diameter and my legs stuck out almost straight to the side. Then he'd heave a big sigh and slowly release his breath. My legs dropped back down to their normal position. Mick did that a couple of times a day. I don't know if he was playing with me or just following some natural urge.

Neil and I were bringing up the rear of the pack when we came across a flock of pink-gray galahs, a pigeon-sized bird known for its stupidity.

"The galah looks a lot like our pigeon, Neil. Are they good eating?" I asked.

"One time we were out on the trail and ran short of food. I clubbed half-a-dozen galahs and roasted them. They turned out to be as tough as saddle leather," Neil explained. "Now I knew the Aborigines ate them so I asked a black fellow how they prepared them.

"He said he roasted them and then filed them into a powder with a coarse rasp, added water and boiled the powder into soup," Neil said with a smile.

"The recipe I heard for cooking galahs," Andrew chimed in, "was to boil six birds and six stones in a pot for six hours. Then you throw the galahs away and eat the stones."

Late in the day we rode up to Renner's Rock, also known as Dr. Stone's Rock. Andrew explained that this was a sacred Aboriginal site. The formation is actually two rocks, each about 40 feet high, connected together. At the base of the larger rock was a small opening, and I mean *small*--about one-foot high and two-feet wide right at ground level. Andrew suggested we crawl in the opening to see the initiation site.

Even though I'm somewhat claustrophobic, I trusted Andrew so I prostrated myself in the dust and wiggled into the opening. With my head sideways so I wouldn't hit it on the top of the rocks I wiggled along the cool, dusty tunnel on my belly with my hands extended out front to feel which way it turned. My body blocked the light from the opening and it was *totally black* in front of me. My heart was pounding a mile-a-minute and I was breathing in short, quick breaths--panic! Then I remembered I still had my small flashlight in its holder on my belt, the one I used to avoid snakes or critters as I went to the outhouse at night. I reached back and pulled it out and switched it on. I could see that a few feet ahead of me the tunnel widened out into a small chamber--probably a ceremonial chamber. As I crawled forward I saw movement off to my left and froze.

"Turn that damn torch off," Neil snapped at me. He had gone around the rock and come in the other side. He was lying in a small chamber off to the left of the tunnel to "ambush" us as we crawled by. I turned the light off and stood up in the inner chamber. One by one the other people crawled into the chamber. As they did, Neil would reach out and grab the unsuspecting victim.

"Ahhhhhhhhhhhh!" was the universal response. Then Neil would identify himself and ask the shaken victim to be quiet. A few minutes later, the next victim would crawl into the darkened chamber and get pounced upon!

After the last of our group experienced the mysterious grabber, I switched on my light to inspect the inner chamber. It was a small, musty room, seven or eight feet high with a chimney opposite where Neil waited for us. The chimney started as a four-foot-high opening in the wall about three feet in diameter. I crouched under the lip and stood up. Shining my light I found the cone-shaped chimney extended 10- or 12-feet up. The opening narrowed quickly. My shoulders were rubbing the sides. I felt that my body was blocking the air from below and I would smother if I stood there very long. Quickly, I wiggled my shoulders loose from the smooth, round hole I was standing in, dropped to my knees and climbed out.

After investigating the remainder of the chamber, we crawled the rest of the way through the rock and came out on the other side. Paul and Nathan enjoyed it so much they crawled through again.

As we continued our ride toward the camel farm, Kelsey, who is a confirmed chocoholic, reminded me that she hadn't had any chocolate for a week. "When we get to the farm you should buy each of us seven Kit Kat bars," she said.

Presently we came to the grain farm across the road from the camel farm.

"This is a highly productive farm," Andrew explained as we rode past a field of oats. "They make use of irrigation to grow up to five rounds of crops a year--oats, sorghum and alfalfa." Off in the field we could see the quarter-mile-long arms of the massive rotating irrigation booms slowly swinging around in a giant green circle.

As we approached the camel farm, Mick, the only bull in our group of 13 camels, started blowing his throat bladder out to impress the females at the farm. He wanted to make sure they recognized him as their leader. The purple bladder was the size of a football. He would blow it out, gurgle and extend his lower lip so he had liver-lips--disgusting to humans, but apparently exhilarating to female camels.

The camels picked up the pace when they smelled the farm and they were almost running as we crossed the highway, rode into the farm yard and headed for the pen.

NOEL FULLERTON'S
SCHOOL OF DROMEDARY SCIENCE

RIGHT AT THE ROCK
DOWN THE ROAD
NEXT TO JIM'S PLACE

DIPLOMA IN CAMELOLOGY

This Certifies that

Kelsey Ann Erickson

has successfully completed a course in Camelology.

Courses Studied : Stage One, Two and Three
of the K-Code of the Camel Handlers Guide to the University
in the state of insanity in the Northern Territory

SORUS BOTTUMUS RIDUS

Signed: *Noel Fullerton*

Dr Chilpy Fullerton C.H.E.
(Camel Handler Extraordinaire)

Each of us received a signed Camel Certificate for successfully completing the safari.

104

"Oosh," I commanded Mick one last time. He knelt obediently and I hopped off. I gave him an affectionate pat and told him what a magnificent camel he was. He stretched his long neck around and rubbed his soft head against my side. Then I collected my backpack, water bottle and camera from the saddle bag, and made sure the grandchildren retrieved their belongings from their saddles.

Kelsey, Tracy and Paul immediately bolted for the gift shop. Pepsis and Kit Kat bars all around. We received a signed certificate declaring we had successfully completed the camel ride. The kids bought some trinkets and I purchased a kilogram of camel down for Gloria to knit into a pair of mittens.

After we finished our shopping we walked back to the pen and said thanks and good-bye to Andrew, Neil and Mel. They did an outstanding job of teaching 10 greenhorns how to ride camels and survive in the desert. Then we hopped on the bus for the ride back to Alice Springs. The group was very subdued during the bus ride--a real letdown after the exciting camel adventure.

I asked the grandchildren what they liked about the trip.

"I liked racing the camels," Kelsey replied with a smile.

"Climbing through the rocks and up to the caves was the best part," Paul said.

"Sitting around the campfire at night and listening to the stories," was Tracy's favorite.

The bus dropped us off at the Territory Motor Inn in Alice Springs. Kelsey, Tracy and Paul immediately went swimming while I washed four loads of clothes. Everything we owned was dirty. That night we lay down in real beds with clean sheets and slept like logs.

CHAPTER 11

AYERS ROCK

"Would you like to drive back to Adelaide rather than fly," I asked, "so that we can climb Ayers Rock and dig for opals at Coober Pedy?"

"Yeah," the grandchildren agreed.

My first problem was finding a car we could rent for the 1,000 mile, one-way drive to Adelaide.

"We don't rent one-way," the Hertz agent told me.

"No cars," the Budget lady said.

"I have an Adelaide car you could take, but the minimum rental is a week," the Territory Rent-A-Car agent replied.

"We'll take it!"

The car turned out to be a right-hand drive, air-conditioned Toyota Camry--very nice. Before we left Alice Springs, we stocked up on cheese, crackers, lunch meat, bread, bottled water, Pepsis, candy bars and ice. With our emergency supplies in hand we drove south along the Stuart Highway toward Ayers Rock.

The temperature was 50F with clear skies--not a cloud in sight. Traffic along Stuart Highway was minimal as we drove through miles of scrub brush, small trees and sand punctuated by an occasional open field with grazing cattle. Grass was so sparse, they often had to cover 25 miles in a day looking for feed. Water troughs were filled from deep wells by windmills.

We visited Ayers Rock after the camel trip.

The cattle soon learned where water was available or they died trying.

"Grandpa, there's some more of those giant eggs alongside the road!" Paul yelled as he pointed out the window.

I slowed the car to a stop and backed up to take another look at the eggs. The "eggs" were the paddy melons we encountered during the camel ride. Sizes varied from tennis balls up to honeydew melons. The smaller melons were perfectly round, but the bigger ones were oblong.

An hour out of Alice Springs we came upon four people taking a noontime camel ride.

"That's our camel farm," Kelsey yelled as we passed Fullerton's. "I don't see Charcoal."

"She's probably already out on another ride."

"Can we stop for ice cream?" Kelsey asked a little later.

The grandchildren resting on way up Ayers Rock.

"Good idea," I agreed.

Right on cue, a gas station and restaurant appeared at the junction of Stuart Highway and Lasseter Highway which led to Ayers Rock.

"They've got a big bird in a cage out back," Kelsey noted as we walked back to the car after lunch and ice cream. We walked around the back to see it.

"It's an emu," I explained.

"It looks like an ostrich, only it's brown" Paul noted.

"They're big," Kelsey said as the emu came over for a handout.

Later, as we crested a hill, Ayers Rock appeared in the distance. Even from 50 miles away it looked big and red.

"How come it's just sitting there all by itself?" Kelsey asked. "Where did it come from?"

Kelsey holding chain as she climbed

"This giant rock, two-miles long, a mile wide and a quarter-mile high; was formed from sediment on the bottom of an ancient sea 600 million years ago," I read from the guide book. "At that time Australia was still connected to South America, Africa and the Antarctic in a supercontinent. About 130 million years ago, the action of the earth's tectonic plates caused Australia to split off the supercontinent and established its own continent. Over the millenniums, the area around Ayers Rock was eroded by water and the wind until the rock eventually fell over to its present position with the sedimentary stripes lying vertical."

"Boy! I'll bet that made a bunch of noise!" Kelsey commented. "I wonder if it landed on anyone?"

"I don't think so. People have only been here about 80,000 years and it fell over long before that."

The grandchildren hid in a cave near the top of Ayers Rock.

Ayers Rock grew bigger and bigger and redder and redder as we drove past Yulara Village and right down to the base of the rock.

"Who owns the rock?" Paul asked as we stopped at the visitor's center.

"The Australian government gave it back to the Aboriginal people, so they own it. The Aborigines consider the rock to be sacred. Their most powerful spirits reside here. They still allow people to climb the rock, but they are concerned the crowds will offend their spirits. Ready to climb?" I asked as I grabbed our water bottle and camera.

"Where do we start?" Tracy asked as we headed for the rock.

We climbed to the top of Ayers Rock in about one hour.

"There's a giant chain anchored along the steepest part of the climb," I said, pointing up to several people holding on to the chain.

"You sure it's safe, grandpa?" Tracy continued.

"They only lose one or two people a year, so we'll be careful."

Paul and Kelsey led the charge up the rock. Tracy and I stopped periodically to rest, but the other two just kept climbing. Paul and Kelsey found a cave in the area where the chain stopped and hid in it.

"Boo!" they yelled as we finally made it to the cave.

As we continued, the route took us over one huge rock mound and down the other side before going up the next mound. Tracy decided to slide down the rocks on her bottom. It didn't work. She wore a big hole in the seat of her sweatpants.

As we climbed down, we couldn't see the bottom of the rock.

Finally reaching the top of the rock, we sat down to rest by a monument.

"The sign says we're at the highest point and shows the direction to the other rocks," Kelsey said as she read the plaque.

A group of French climbers joined us. I asked one of them if he would take a photo of the four of us standing by the monument to document our achievement.

We drank the rest of our water and started the climb down. I followed the white line indicating the preferred path, but Paul, Tracy and Kelsey decided to go up and down the steeper sections in a straight line. We made it down in record time--about an hour and a half round-trip. The park ranger told us the normal round-trip time was two or three hours.

The sun was low in the sky so we quickly drove to the viewing area to take pictures of the rock. Ayers Rock turned brighter and brighter red as the sun set.

We drove to Yulara Village, a modern tourist complex about five miles from Ayers Rock. Hundreds of white canvas sails provided shade for the treeless compound and a festive atmosphere. With the aid of a map, I finally located our Emu Walk apartment in the maze of colorful buildings. The apartment consisted of one bedroom, a living room, kitchen and bath. Tracy and Kelsey opted to sleep on the pullout bed in the living room because the TV was in there. Paul and I chose the bedroom.

"What's for supper?" Kelsey asked.

"Let's walk down to the restaurant and see," I suggested.

There were several restaurants available, but the grandchildren chose the fast-food one--surprise!

"Two chicken dinners and two fish dinners," I told the lady at the cash register.

We ate back in the apartment so the grandchildren could watch TV and relax. Everyone was tired from the drive and the climb.

I made reservations for a starlight walk and a star show, but I wasn't sure I could keep everyone awake until it started. Fortunately, the grandchildren were interested enough in the TV program that they stayed awake until bus time. At 8:30, we caught the bus to the observatory on the edge of the village.

Half a dozen telescopes were set up there along with some gas heaters, since it became very cold after the sun went down. The guide/astronomer related the story of the universe, pointing out the Milky Way which stood out brightly against the clear, dark skies around Ayers Rock. The crescent of the planet Venus was clearly visible through the telescopes. I had to keep coaxing Kelsey away from the gas heater to view the heavens. She was cold! For the first time in my life I saw the four moons around Jupiter and could even see the blemish on the surface of Jupiter caused by a comet collision. The guide pointed out the Southern Cross and various constellations. The night air grew colder and colder making it more and more difficult to get Kelsey, Paul and Tracy away from the gas heaters. They served us a cup of hot tea and some cookies which warmed everyone up. It was 10:30 when we arrived back at the apartment. The kids wanted to go to bed with their clothes on. Everyone crashed.

Just before sunrise I made a cup of tea and sat on the porch enjoying the early-morning solitude of the desert. Nothing was stirring. Then I heard the mynah birds come to life. They sang their beautiful 13 or 14 note repertoire trying to raise the sun. After their rendition, the sun moved up a little. The mynah birds sang their melodious song a little louder and a little prettier. Each time they did, the sun moved up a little more. Finally after five or six tries, they raised the sun completely above the horizon. The exhausted mynahs then became completely silent--no more singing until later in the day.

While my exhausted grandchildren slept, I drove back down to Ayers Rock for an early morning run around that beautiful backdrop. As I ran on that cool, clear morning, I distinctly heard a cryptic chanting. I couldn't see anyone within a mile in front or back of me, yet I could clearly hear male voices talking in a tongue I didn't recognize. Mile after mile, minute after minute, the voices continued and always as loud as if they were standing 10 or 15 feet away. When I finally arrived back at the car, I met a group of early morning climbers and asked if they had heard the voices.

"What voices?" was the reply.

Where were the voices coming from? Ayers Rock is sacred to the Aborigines, full of spirits and mythology. The ranger said they were from people on top of the rock whose voices, by a quirk of nature, rolled down the side of the rock. Maybe they came from the sacred Aboriginal spirits in the rock.

"Can we go to the gift shop?" Kelsey asked after breakfast.

"Sure." We drove to the visitor's center and watched Aborigines women painting their traditional pictures of symmetrical patterns of brightly colored dots or dots outlining a snake or kangaroo. Some of the women were carving wood while others were painting the finished carvings. The designs were unique and very attractive.

We bought several postcards of Aboriginal art and then drove 30 miles to the Olgas, a series of rocks similar to Ayers Rock, except they haven't fallen over yet. The strata are still horizontal as they originally were. The Olgas consist of several dozen separate red rocks rising from the desert floor. They appear to be parts of some giant, buried mythical creature.

"Can we climb them?" Kelsey asked.

"Sure. Why not?"

We followed a path leading between two of the giant rocks and Paul discovered a cave 50 feet up the sheer side of one rock.

"Let's go up there," Paul said. He searched for hand holds in the steep face of the rock. Slowly and steadily he climbed up and up until he disappeared into the 10-foot diameter cave. Tracy followed his every move until she was 25 feet up the wall and got stuck. I climbed up behind her to help while Paul coached her from above. With Paul's help, she made it into the cave. Then I went back down and helped Kelsey up the sheer wall. Kids are fearless. In a few minutes we were all sitting in the cave. The smooth, dry cave was only five-feet deep. The back wall was covered with Aboriginal spiral drawings and sunbursts.

Tracy and Kelsey climbing up to a cave in the Olgas.

"How are we going to get down?" Tracy asked. She looked out the cave entrance at the sheer vertical wall below. It was one thing to climb when we could look up to find the next hand/foot hold, but looking down a sheer 50-foot cliff was terrifying. Kelsey decided she couldn't get down.

"Could you go get a rope or ladder or something?" she asked.

"No, we'll just leave you here," I said.

"Mommy will be mad," Kelsey responded.

She was right. I climbed down first and stopped about five feet below the cave floor. Paul then lowered Kelsey down to me. I found her a couple of handholds and a foothold. Then I climbed down another five feet and Kelsey slid down to where I was. I caught her and secured her on handholds and footholds. After several such maneuvers we arrived at the gentler slope and she climbed down the rest of the way herself. With Kelsey safe, I climbed back up and helped Tracy down. Paul scrambled down like the experienced rock climber he is.

After exploring the Olgas, we drove back to Ayers Rock. As I made a turn, I saw a long, brown snake stretched across the road. I swerved, but still ran over it.

"It's still wiggling," Kelsey said as she looked back.

"The locals say it will wiggle until sundown," I said.

A little further on a dingo ran across the road in front of us and almost knocked over a shingle-backed lizard who was sitting at the roadside with its gaping mouth open, hissing. Nearby we passed a flock of crested doves. There were also flocks of rosellas, a white bird with a pink head and flocks of pink and gray galahs. Plenty of food for the dingos, snakes and lizards.

CHAPTER 12

COOBER PEDY

We left Ayers Rock and headed south on Stuart Highway towards Coober Pedy late Tuesday morning.

"What's a Coober Pedy?" Kelsey asked when I told her our destination.

"It's an Aboriginal expression meaning 'white man's burrow'," I said.

"Why did they call it that?" Kelsey asked.

"They dig for opal in Coober Pedy. There are thousands of holes, or burrows, in the ground."

"How did they find the opal there?" Paul asked.

"Opal was first discovered at Coober Pedy in 1915 by some prospectors traveling west looking for gold. The prospectors discovered several loose opals in the riverbed. They followed the opal trail upstream until they found a vein of opal on an exposed ledge near what would become Coober Pedy. That vein produced some of the finest gem-quality opal ever mined."

"Are opals found anywhere else?" Tracy asked.

"Opal is relatively common and found all over the world, but 90 percent of the gem-quality opal is found in Australia at places with colorful names like Lightning Ridge, White Cliffs, Tintinbar and Coober Pedy. Coober Pedy produces more opal than all the rest of Australia combined."

"Look at the big birds," Kelsey said, pointing ahead of the car.

Four huge wedge-tailed eagles sat on the ground and in a tree. They spread their wings and took off in graceful flight as we drove by.

Near Kulgera we drove through some huge red sandstone rock formations.

"I can see Ayers Rock," Tracy said. It did look like a half-scale version of Ayers Rock.

"Why is the dirt red?" Kelsey asked.

"It's rich in iron oxide," I replied.

"There's a dead cow in the ditch," Paul noted.

The cow had been hit by a car. Several dingoes and a couple of vultures were eating the carcass. It looked like a scene from an African nature movie. The dingoes and vultures scattered as we drove by.

There wasn't much traffic on the highway. About half of the vehicles we saw were pulling travel trailers or caravans as the Australians call them.

"We should rent a trailer," Tracy suggested. "That way we wouldn't have to pay for a motel every night."

"You guys like the pool at the motels. It would be difficult swimming in the back of a travel trailer."

"Naw," Paul replied. "We could jump off the toilet into the bathtub."

We stopped at a truck layby for a comfort break and to snack on our picnic supplies. The layby consisted of a large gravel lot with no buildings, but a good hilltop view of the desert. After lunch I let Paul, who was 14 years old, drive the car around the truck layby to see what a right-hand drive car felt like. He did a surprisingly good job.

As we drove on, the highway appeared deserted. It was as if we were the last people on earth, driving forever on a dead planet. Other than the scrub brush, there were no signs of life. We passed no other roads, houses nor farms, and saw no other people. It was 100 miles between towns--not a good place for the car to break down. Whenever we encountered a gas station I stopped just to convince myself that there really were people out there.

At Marla Bore we stopped for gas and ice cream. I went in what appeared to be the post office to buy stamps for our postcards.

"Can I get stamps here?" I asked.

"No," the lady behind the counter replied. "This is the motel reception desk. You have to go to the post office around the corner." She pointed out the door and motioned around to the left.

I walked out the door and around the corner into the post office. There was no one behind the counter. A minute later the motel receptionist walked through the door connecting the motel to the post office. Small town--she was the motel receptionist and the postmistress; she sold me the stamps and took my postcards to mail.

Outside of town we scared up a flock of about a hundred sulphur-crested cockatoos sitting alongside the road. Beautifully colored birds. Then we came to the dog fence. There are dingo fences all around South Australia to protect the sheep country from the dingoes. They are allowed to run wild in the Northern Territory and West Australia where they raise cattle, but not in South Australia.

Near Coober Pedy the flat, featureless desert gave way to big mounds of dirt piled alongside thousands of vertical mine shafts. Huge, deep scars appeared in the desert floor where the miners bulldozed the rock and dirt to expose the opal bearing strata.

We arrived in Coober Pedy late in the afternoon. The town was located in the middle of an inhospitable desert--no water, no shade, no wood and extreme heat. The average daily summer temperature in Coober Pedy is 115 degrees. Fortunately, our visit occurred during the Australian winter and temperatures were only in the 90s. Because of the intense heat and lack of building materials, many of the town's residents live in dugouts--

We saw dirt piled around thousands of vertical opal-mine shafts near Coober Pedy.

shelters carved out of the hillside. The post office, Catholic church, bank, restaurants and three motels are all underground, as is 40 percent of the private housing.

Even in the middle of the Australian winter, Coober Pedy looks dried out and dusty with piles of junk machinery lying everywhere. The buildings were one-story and minimal. The tour book described the town as "a good place to stop for gas, but best suited for miners, would-be ants and movie companies." The movie "Mad Max III" was filmed here because the area looked like the end of the earth. The population of 2,100 people is composed of 53 different nationalities with a reputation for volatility--one tough town. Almost every vehicle in town has an "explosives" sign on it. The drive-in movie posted a notice: "Patrons are not to bring dynamite to the movies."

The intense summer heat caused many people to live in underground houses.

I had booked us into a dugout motel. Our accommodations were carved out of the gypsum rock with a mine tunneling machine. The temperature remains 70 degrees year-round in the cave--no need for heaters or air conditioning.

In the bathroom was a sign, *"Please conserve water-- take a bath with a friend!"*

"How come we have to conserve water?" Kelsey asked. "I thought there was water everywhere!"

"Not everywhere," I said. "Rainfall here is only a few inches per year. Water rationing has always been a way of life here. It used to be trucked in from McDougall Peak Homestead, 80 miles away. In the 1960s each white resident was limited to 20 gallons of water a week for washing, cooking and drinking. Baths were prohibited. The Aboriginal natives were allowed

Even the Catholic church is built underground.

10 gallons a week. The ration was increased to 150 gallons a week in the early 1980s. A new water plant was completed a few years later that draws saline water from 100 meters below the surface and runs it through a complex, reverse osmosis process to provide a sufficient supply of potable water so rationing is no longer needed. Water is still expensive at $40 for 1,000 gallons."

"Is it okay if I drink a glass of water?" Kelsey asked.

"Yes, you can drink as much as you like."

After unloading our luggage, we walked down the street to an old opal mine. The owners had converted it to an opal shop. First we looked around their showroom and then walked down into one of the opal mine tunnels. The mine tunnel was lit with black lights and the veins of opal glowed with brilliant fluorescent colors. Paul's shirt also glowed as though he had a light inside him. The fringe on Tracy's jacket and Kelsey's shirt also glowed.

After walking through the mine, we watched a video that explained opal mining.

Opal occurs in thin seams or veins of clay-bearing matrix. These veins slope down from the exposed ridge where the original discovery occurred in 1915. At most locations the vein lies 10 to 50 feet below the surface, under layers of sandstone, gravel and solid rock. The typical recovery process is to dig a vertical shaft about three feet in diameter, hauling the debris to the surface in buckets with a power winch. When the solid rock "shincracker" layer is encountered, explosives are used to blast through the five- to ten-foot thick layers. Once the clay "opal dirt" layer is reached, the miner digs horizontally under a roof of rock with a two-pound pick looking for nodules of opal. Light is provided with electric torches or candles stuck in an iron spike called a "spider."

Opal is more scarce than diamonds, but because the opal market is not controlled (the diamonds are controlled by the powerful De Beers cartel that only allows so many on the market at a time), opal prices are not as high as diamonds. The black opal from Lightning Ridge sells for about $400 a carat raw and $1,000 a carat polished and set. The light colored opal from Coober Pedy only brings about $10 a carat in the field and $25 a carat polished and set. Because of the limited mining techniques used, it is estimated that only about 2 percent of the opal in Coober Pedy has been recovered to date. The current opal output runs around $2 million a year.

Most gemstones such as rubies and diamonds are crystalline in form with an orderly repeated molecular structure that generates plane faces in a symmetrical arrangement. Opal in contrast is amorphous, without definite shape. The gem is similar to glass in form and composed of silicon dioxide. In past eons, water dissolved the silica to form a silica gel. This then seeped into cracks formed by earth movements as the earth's crust cooled

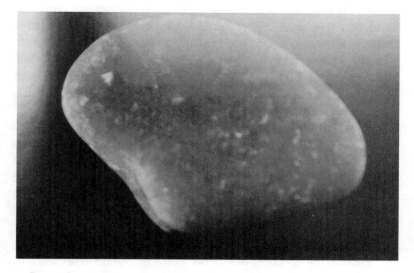

Sometimes the opal replaces the calcium in a scallop shell.

and buckled. Over time, the silica gel hardened and formed thin layers of opal. These layers vary from a fraction of an inch to several inches thick. Opal is also found in fossils of shells, bones and trees. The original shells from an inland sea were covered with layers of sand and limestone. Water leaching through the sandstone dissolved the calcium of the shell, leaving a void in the shape of the shell. The silica gel seeping through the sandstone filled the void and solidified, creating opalized scallop shells.

   The color of crystal gemstones comes from the minute impurities that are present to form, for example, the pink of rose quartz. In quartz, the color process is due to filtration. Only the pink portion of the white light passes through the quartz. The color of opal is produced in a different way--by diffraction. The silicon dioxide molecules form miniature spheres of various sizes. If a group of similar size spheres line up in a regular arrangement, they produce a three-dimensional diffraction grating that splits the incident white light into its component colors. Large spheres produce all the colors of the rainbow from red through green to violet. Intermediate size spheres display green to violet while small spheres produce only violet. If the size or arrangement of the spheres are irregular, the resultant color is milky or white, resulting in low-value opals called "potch."

"Let's go to the gift shop," Kelsey suggested.

From the extensive collection of opal items, Tracy picked an opal bookmark, Kelsey bought an opal pin and Paul bought a long, thin tube of beautiful green and blue opals displayed in water. Then we went out in front of the shop and dug through barrels of mine tailing, looking for opal. Every one of the grandchildren found pieces of opal--maybe not gem quality, but an authentic Australian opal! After digging through the barrels, we drove to the outskirts of Coober Pedy and climbed up some of the mine tailings and searched for pay-dirt there. Again, the grandchildren were lucky enough to find some beautiful gypsum crystals and small pieces of brightly colored opal.

On the way back to town I stopped in the grocery store to buy some picture postcards of the area. While looking around I struck up a conversation with an elderly miner who was shopping for essentials--beer.

"Coober Pedy has gotten too civilized," he said shaking his head. "Used to be only two policemen. On Saturday night us miners would get drunk and they'd get drunk and nobody bothered nobody. Now there are 10 policemen and they'll arrest you for just having a good time!"

"Are there many fights in Coober Pedy nowadays?" I asked.

"Yeah, there's still some good fights," he explained. "Just last week a couple of guys had a disagreement about the ownership of a particular mining claim. They both ended up with big ears and free accommodations for the night," he said with a smile.

"What's for supper?" Tracy asked when we arrived back at our motel.

"I'm having a kangaroo steak," I said after looking at the menu.

"Not me," Tracy replied. The grandchildren ordered pizza. No sense of adventure. The kangaroo steak was as tasty as beef, but a little tougher.

"Can we play cards?" Kelsey asked after supper.

We played UNO until everyone was tired. When I finally turned out the lights in our cave (room) it was *totally dark* and *totally quiet!*

"It's too dark in here," Kelsey said less than a minute later. "Can you leave a night-light on?" I switched on the bathroom light and left the door ajar.

"Did you enjoy your stay?" Mrs. Radeka, the motel owner's wife, asked the next morning.

"Oh, yes!" I replied enthusiastically. "We found a bit of opal, slept in a dugout, ate kangaroo steaks for supper and saw some fantastic country. If only it weren't so hot!"

"Hot? This ain't hot, mate," Mrs. Radeka said with a grin. "If you was here a few months ago, you'd know what hot was. Why it was so hot you'da thought we was next door to hell and all the fences was down!"

After a hearty breakfast of Weet-Bix we headed down Stuart Highway for Adelaide. The terrain south of Coober Pedy was very flat. There were no trees, just one-foot-high salt grass for mile after mile.

Look at that sign!" Kelsey yelled as she pointed to a highway sign warning of camel, wombat and kangaroo crossing for the next 96 kilometers.

**We passed a road sign warning of camel, wombat and
kangaroo crossing.**

"There's a hawk!" Paul called out. It was sitting at the
side of the road on a rock with his back to the sun. He had his
wings and tail-feathers spread out as though he were in flight.
The hawk was drying his feathers and warming up his body in the
sun.

There was still very little traffic on the highway. I could
drive in high gear for about 250 miles without ever having to take
my foot off the gas. We sang and played "I see something white"
games to pass the time.

"Look at the big bird," Kelsey yelled as we drove past a
pair of emus walking beside the road. I pulled over by Lake Hart
and took out my camera. Lake Hart is one of the saltwater lakes
near Woormera. Once we stopped, I realized there were dozens
of emus there. One of the males darted across the road. His mate

128

was reluctant to cross. She ran nervously up to the edge of the road and then ran back trying to coax her mate back to her side of the road. With the female coaxing him on, the male finally decided to come back across the highway. Bad timing! A big truck was roaring down the highway. The truck driver slammed on his brakes and brought the truck to a skidding, screeching halt as the emu ambled back across the road and joined his nervous mate. Emus are not very bright birds.

The telephone company laid a fiber optic cable from Adelaide through Alice Springs to Darwin and over to Indonesia. About every 40 miles along the road we saw repeater-stations that amplified the telephone signals and sent them on. They consisted of a six-foot-square cement-block hut with no windows. There were two solar panels on the roof powering the fiber optic repeaters. The solar panels charged up the batteries so the telephone signals could be amplified.

We passed through Woomera which was home to the South Australia rocket range and a secret satellite tracking and control station. Big signs warned "Entry into the Woomera Rocket Range is prohibited!" During the Cold War days of the 1960s and 70s, Woomera was very active, but has been closed for the past 10 years. There is talk about reactivating it now that telephone companies are planning to launch hundreds of communications satellites in the next few years.

The Flinders Ranges appeared on the eastern horizon shortly after we passed Woomera. We drove into beautiful Port Augusta, the northern port on the Spencer Gulf in the early afternoon. It was a shock to see green trees, grass and flowers in town after driving through 1,000 miles of desert. At Port Augusta's post office, I bought a money order to send for the Rainbow Valley topographical maps and mailed it to the Land Management Office in Alice Springs. That office wasn't open when we left there.

South of Port Augusta, the traffic picked up noticeably as we entered the more populated portion of South Australia. There are continuous streams of cars coming and going. Houses, farms, gas stations and businesses appeared along the road. We arrived at the Greenwood Apartments in Adelaide about supper time--a long day's drive.

CHAPTER 13

THE GREAT BARRIER REEF

We were up at dawn for our trip to the Great Barrier Reef. I dropped the rental car at the airport; then we cooled our heels waiting for our flight to Sydney. The Sydney air traffic controllers were staging a slow down. Like our U.S. air traffic controllers, the Australian controllers are not allowed to strike. Instead, they stage traffic slow downs and hope the inconvenienced air travelers will be sympathetic to their cause. I didn't feel much sympathy as we waited two hours in the airport for our flight. However, it did give us time for a leisurely breakfast and a little shopping.

The Sydney controllers finally released our flight. The grandchildren napped on the flight while Gloria and I marveled at the changing landscape between Adelaide and Sydney--fields of brown wheat, yellow sour sop, purple salvation jane; the green woods; muddy rivers and mountains. We changed planes in Sydney and again in Brisbane. It took all day to fly the 2,000 miles of Cairns, Queensland. Our final destination was Port Douglas, 40 miles north to Cairns. With the good services of the Coral Coach Line, we headed for Port Douglas.

The one-hour drive was breathtaking--white-capped waves from the deep-blue South Pacific Ocean pounded the shore on one side of the road and the green Australian mountains rose majestically on the other. It was a completely different world from Alice Springs and the desert. Cairns is at the edge of a tropical rain forest. All the rain that doesn't fall in Alice Springs falls in Cairns. The mountains had rugged slopes and sharp peaks covered with trees and lush vegetation.

"Look at all the smoke," Kelsey said, pointing to a forest fire burning high up in the mountains.

131

It was about 8 p.m. when the Coral Coach dropped us off at the Nimrod Apartments in Port Douglas. Our apartment resembled a Hollywood movie set! The three-bedroom apartment occupied the entire top floor of the unit. There was a full-length porch in back and a two-thirds length porch on the front side. Each bedroom had a door opening onto the porch. There was a large living room, a spacious dining area, full kitchen, washer/dryer utility room and a bath-and-a-half. The master bath opened directly into the master bedroom and also into the hall.

"We've died and gone to heaven," Kelsey yelled as she explored all the potential hiding places for her favorite game-- hide-and-seek.

Gloria and I sat on the back porch enjoying the tropical breeze and watched the golden rays of the beautiful equatorial sunset through the gently swaying palm trees. Pinch me, I think I'm dreaming. The grandchildren ran down to check out the pool and then played cards till bedtime.

I jogged down to the beach just before sunrise the next morning to explore the surroundings. After the first mile, I cut back to the main road to see what was there. A general store materialized along my route so I bought groceries for breakfast and lunch.

Gloria and I enjoyed a leisurely breakfast and then sat on the porch, talked and drank a cup of tea. The grandchildren slept till 7:30 or 8:00, ate their breakfast and we headed for the ocean.

"The water is too cold to swim," Kelsey said as we waded through the surf. "Let's collect shells."

There were thousands of tropical seashells on Four-Mile Beach. The smooth, white-sand beach extended four miles without a house, dock, buildings or lifeguard shack--just golden sand with palm and small mangrove trees growing on this incredible beach. All the houses were set back several hundred feet behind the trees so we couldn't see a single one from the

At Four-Mile Beach in Queensland, the grandchildren hunted for shells.

beach. It looked like a deserted tropical beach--one of the most beautiful ones I've ever seen.

The grandchildren ran back to the apartment about noon carrying their bag of shells and jumped in the swimming pool. The pool was 150 feet long with a dog-leg bend and bridge in the middle. It had a gentle slope from very shallow at one end to eight-foot deep at the other end. Perfect water temperature-- refreshing, but not cold. There was also a hot-tub/whirlpool alongside the main pool. The grandchildren loved it! They all tried out their snorkels and masks. I took some underwater photos of Paul swimming along the bottom and of a headless Kelsey. The reflection from the water surface gave the illusion of a headless body standing in the pool.

Paul spent all day at the beach or in the pool.

Kelsey, Tracy, Paul and I walked back to the ocean after lunch. The tide was *waaaaay* out. The flat sand beach now extended 300 yards further out than it did at 10 a.m. What a difference the tide makes. We waded out through a few puddles and finally started swimming when the water was waist deep. Much to my surprise, the water was dirty. I could only see a foot or two underwater with my mask and snorkel. Apparently run-off from the torrential equatorial rains carried the dirt into the ocean.

Kelsey had a great time jumping in the *"tidal waves,"* as she called them. She would emit a blood-curdling yell every time a wave came in. Paul and Tracy splashed around and played tag. After an hour in the waves, everyone walked back to the beach. Paul hunted for shells while Tracy, Kelsey and I built a sandcastle. I was 58-years old at the time and that was the first sandcastle I'd ever completed. Oh, I'd messed around with castles

Kelsey became *headless* when viewed from underwater.

before and built little bits, but had never really completed an elaborate sandcastle. With the help of Kelsey and Tracy, we built a deluxe castle consisting of four turrets, a moat, a wall around the moat, two drawbridges, a summer house, school, a grocery store outside and a road leading from the sandcastle all the way out to the ocean. We decorated the sandcastle with seashells which Paul supplied. If I say so myself, it was a beautiful sandcastle--a work of art!

For supper we dined on carry-out pizza, deep-fried shrimp and fish filets--a gourmet treat. Then Kelsey and Tracy cut out and colored paper dolls. Paul arranged his shell collection. He had picked up over 150 beautiful shells from the beach. Some still had hermit crabs living inside them. Paul sorted the shells--one bucket for shells with live crabs and another for empty shells. Then he put the empty shells in the bathtub and washed them off until they were all shiny and clean. The live shells remained on the front porch.

There was a Simpson brand washer and dryer in the apartment, spelled like the Simpson Desert. I washed several loads of clothes while we were there. The machine had a unique personality; it washed in slow motion. The agitator went *rooor, rooor, rooor*, pause, *rooor, rooor, rooor*, pause, *rooor, rooor, rooor*, pause, for about 15 minutes during the wash cycle. Then it started to spin. It wound itself up like an airplane propeller--

rrrrr rrrrr rrrrr rrrrr rrrrr **rrrrr** **rrrrr** **rrrrr**

rrrrr rrrrr rrrrr rrrrr. It must

have reached a thousand-rpm before it stopped roaring. The clothes came out clean, but the noise was nerve-wracking.

Our trip out to the Great Barrier Reef was scheduled for the next day. Before I came to Australia, I thought the Barrier Reef started at the beach and extended out a mile or so as the reef does at Waikiki Beach in Hawaii. Not true. The Great Barrier Reef lays 50 to 150 miles from shore at the edge of the continental shelf. It wasn't even visible from shore! This day we would ride the Quicksilver out to the reef. Quicksilver was a giant stainless-steel catamaran, about 100-foot long and designed to carry 150 people. The twin hulls were shaped like torpedoes so they would pierce the waves rather than ride up and down on the tops. The catamaran boasted a top speed of 28 knots, covering the 50-mile ride to the reef in about two hours.

The seas were quite rough. The crew suggested everyone take seasick pills that they offered--most everyone did. The winds were about 25 knots and the boat rolled around side-to-side. Several people suffered "mal de mar"; fortunately none from the Johnson group.

During the ride out, a marine biologist gave us a lecture on the history and makeup of the Great Barrier Reef. It's the longest coral reef in the world—2,300 kilometers long, situated on the edge of the continental shelf of Eastern Australia--50 to 150 miles off land. The reef is several million years old; though the current living reef is much younger. During the last Ice Age 18,000 years ago, the ocean level was 300-feet below the current sea level. The water was trapped as ice at the poles. The entire reef was exposed to the sun and died. At the end of the Ice Age, the reef was reflooded as the ice melted. New coral started building again on top of the old coral. Therefore, the live portion of this magnificent coral reef is only about 10-thousand years old.

The Great Barrier Reef is not one continuous, long reef. It is a series of separate ribbon reefs or islands. Outside the reef, the ocean drops quickly to a depth of one-and-a-half miles, while inside the reef the continental shelf is only 20- to 100-feet deep. The top of the reef is flat and varies in width from a few feet to a mile. At low tide, the top of the reef is exposed a few feet above the water. At high tide, the reef is a few feet beneath the water.

Coral itself is a little animal, a polyp. It gets most of its energy from little one-celled plants which are actually under its skin that photosynthesize the sunlight and generate sugars and starches to feed the polyp. The coral polyps live in colonies and builds a reef from the limestone skeleton of the colony. One colony may measure three to six feet in diameter. It attaches to another colony and continues to build the reef. The coral polyps reproduce by splitting into two; one half floats away to establish itself somewhere else and another coral colony is established.

There are about 300 kinds of coral making up the Great Barrier Reef. Since the coral splits in two, the new polyp is genetically identical to the one that it left. In order to allow genetic evolution, once a year the coral actually produces sperm and eggs that rise to the surface and float to some other part of the reef. There, another coral colony is begun. With new eggs and sperm it is possible for the coral to evolve to meet changing environmental conditions.

The fish love to eat the sperm and the eggs. To defend themselves, *the coral colonies all release their eggs on the same day.* How so many single-cell polyps are able to set their clocks and all release at the same time is a mystery. Miraculously, on the fourth day after the full moon in the month of *November all the coral polyps along the entire 2,300 kilometer reef release their eggs and sperm.* One giant sexual orgy! The entire area is flooded with eggs and sperm. The fish eat the eggs, but there are so many that they cannot possibly consume them all. About half of the sperm and eggs survive.

The entire reef area is protected as the Great Barrier Reef Marine Reserve. About 70 percent of the reef is open to the public and to commercial fishing. It is one of the most abundant fishing areas in the world, but very delicate. The remaining 30 percent of the reef is closed to people and exploitation. The commission is trying very hard to make maximum use of the reef

138

by allowing people to continue to fish, swim and dive on various parts of it.

One of the biggest hazards to the reef is pollution coming from the mainland as agricultural chemicals. Fertilizers wash into the sea and are trapped in the lagoon. The effect on the reef can be devastating. The local governments are trying to clean up the rivers to avoid destruction of the reef. It is a very active ecological area and they are trying to maintain the balance and allow commercial fishing and exploitation. More and more people are visiting the reef and the ecological pressure is increasing. We were not allowed to take any fish, shells or coral from the reef. Look but don't touch! The Reef Commission patrols the reef with boats and planes to make sure that people follow the rules.

After the lecture on the reef, Kelsey, Tracy, Paul and I went up on the top deck to enjoy the fresh air. The boat was traveling 28 knots into a 25-knot head wind. The effect was exciting--like standing on the wing of a plane while it was flying—al la Titanic. The boat pitched while it rolled back and forth. We were about 30-feet above the water on a large lever arm, swinging back and forth like an amusement-park ride. The kids thought it was fun. Adults threw up. After two hours of this exciting ride, we arrived at Agin Court Reef, one of the ribbon reefs along the outer edge of the continental shelf. They docked the Quicksilver against a pontoon platform that was permanently moored on the reef.

The platform consisted of a big covered picnic area, a couple of ramps for submersibles to pull up alongside, and ramps to launch divers. The diver ramps were reached by a set of stairs that led to a platform floor about two feet under the water. I walked down the stairs into the ocean and sat down on the bench to put on my fins and mask, stood up, stepped forward and fell into the water--very neat system.

139

A huge parrot fish swam by me at the Great Barrier Reef.

Kelsey could swim, but the ocean intimidated her so she played on the ramp. She put her mask and snorkel on and swam in the waist-deep water.

Tracy, Paul and I dove in the ocean. Tracy swam close to the ramps since she was not a very strong swimmer and there was quite a strong current on the reef. The tide was coming in and if Paul and I lay still in the water, the current washed us toward the shore at a couple of knots. We had to swim continuously towards the reef if we wanted to stay in one place and look at the fish or coral.

The fish knew that people came to the pontoon each day. To get a free meal, the fish need only to swim around the pontoon, look pretty and pose for a few photos. The view of the green, orange, iridescent-blue and yellow tropical fish around the pontoon was fantastic. We saw three-foot-long parrot fish, giant rainbow-colored fish, little black and white zebra fish and three or four dozen other varieties close to the pontoon. Brain corals, stag corals, fan corals and a dozen other varieties I couldn't name grew on the reef. The coral varied from bright blue to brown, red and green.

I decided to swim from the pontoon lagoon out to the edge of the coral. I swam and swam and swam and swam against the current and only made it half way to the shallow part of the reef. Since I wasn't making much headway, I turned around and let the current sweep me back to the pontoon. Great fun.

For the non-swimmers like Gloria, they had a submersible boat where the pilot remained in a cockpit above the waterline. The passengers climbed down into a viewing section 10-feet below the water level. The pilot drove the submersible around the reef so the passengers could view the fish, coral and giant clams. Paul, Tracy, Kelsey, Gloria and I took a half-hour ride in this great invention.

One of the most interesting things we saw was the giant clam. These creatures weigh about 500 pounds and have a bright-colored mantel sticking out of the slightly-open shell. The clams sucked in water and algae, then spewed out a cloud of debris. Their intake was at the edge of the mantel; the exhaust was in the center. The clams measured three-feet across. They were like the ones from the old John Wayne movies where the pearl diver's foot gets stuck as the shell closes. That doesn't really happen. The clam closes its shell slowly, taking a full minute. The idea of someone getting a leg caught in a clam is Hollywood fiction.

There are 1,600 varieties of fish on the coral reef. We saw about 50 different kinds swimming around the pontoon. One was a little, fluorescent orange and white cleaner fish that ate the parasites off the bigger fish. It actually swam into the mouth of the sea trout and cleaned around the teeth and gills. For some reason, the sea trout loses its aggressiveness when the small fish is at work. A giant ray came swimming by. The cleaning fish abandoned the other fish in the area and headed for the ray. As many as 50 of these little fish scurried around the giant ray eating the parasites from it. The marine biologist told us that the cleaning fish is one of the most important fish in the area because it keeps the reef fish healthy.

Several white-tipped sharks swam by as we explored the reef. They were only three-foot long. The sharks were more interested in small fish than people; not very aggressive. Fortunately, we didn't see any tiger sharks or great whites.

A zillion sea birds circled around the pontoon. Schools of small fish swam near the surface of the ocean to avoid the big, hungry fish. The sea birds would swoop down and snatch them from the water. All of God's creatures have to eat.

I encountered several huge, blue-green fish that weighed at least 100 pounds. They were four-feet long and almost two-feet high from the bottom fin to the top.

Paul, Tracy and I were in and out of the water for three hours--swimming, eating lunch and swimming again. The staff provided a tasty smorgasbord with shrimp, chicken, rice, salad and fruit--all you could eat. The boiled shrimp still had the heads on. Tracy had never seen a whole shrimp before.

"Can I take one home to show mom what a shrimp looks like in the wild?" Tracy asked.

"I don't think so."

"Where do the shrimp come from?" Kelsey asked.

"The ocean," I said.

"You mean like right here?"

"Could be."

"I'm not going back in the ocean," Kelsey replied. "I don't want to meet any shrimp."

"This chicken also comes from the ocean," I joked.

"The ocean?" Kelsey asked skeptically.

"Yeah, it is a special salt-water chicken."

"I don't think so," Kelsey replied. She's gullible, but not dumb.

Four hours after we arrived, the captain tooted the boat's whistle. Everyone swam back to the boat and the captain pushed off for shore. After changing clothes we snacked on cookies, cheese and crackers. Kelsey and Tracy slept most of the way back, exhausted.

"Can we go to the beach?" Kelsey asked when the tour bus dropped us off at our apartment.

The tide had destroyed our sandcastle. Tracy and Kelsey started to build a bigger and better one. They used the sand bucket as a mold to build the walls so they had continuous turrets going down each side. We worked on the castle until dark.

That evening I sat reading Robyn Davidson's book *Tracks* about her trip from Alice Springs to the sea with four camels and a dog (Davidson, 1980).

"Some lady rode a camel across the desert by herself?" Kelsey asked when she saw the picture on the cover.

"She set out with her camels from near Alice Springs and rode west 1,700 miles until she came to the ocean," I replied. "An elderly Aboriginal man rode along for part of the trip. He taught her to find food and water in the desert." I read excerpts of the book to the grandchildren. They were impressed that a lady could survive in the desert by herself.

"I wouldn't want to be out there by myself," Tracy said.

"Me neither," Kelsey echoed.

We sat on the porch before bedtime reminiscing with the grandchildren about the day's reef adventures. I could see Kelsey was preoccupied. Finally she asked, "Grandpa, how long would it take to build a sandcastle we could get inside?"

"About a week," I guessed.

"How much longer are we gonna be here?"

"Two more days."

"Oh," she shrugged. "I'd sure like to build a big castle I could get inside."

The next morning Kelsey brought up the idea again of building a giant sandcastle with walls four-feet high. She agreed it didn't need a roof, but she wanted high walls. We walked to the beach where Kelsey and Tracy drew the outline in the sand. Ten-feet long by eight-feet wide. Kelsey started building the walls with buckets of sand. She was having trouble getting all the sand out of the bucket. The wet sand stuck to the bottom, making only half a turret per bucket.

"Sprinkle some dry sand in the bucket first then pack it with wet sand," I said.

Kelsey walked up on the shore and picked up three buckets of dry sand. She prepared the bucket before putting the wet sand in. The sand came out perfectly each time. She decided she needed a turret every two feet down each side of the wall. She made the turrets and I filled in the walls between.

"Make the walls square with places where they can shoot their arrows out," Kelsey said.

I built a wall two-thirds the height of the tower and used a stick to make depressions in the walls for the arrow shooters. Meanwhile, Tracy was digging the moat. She dug it two-feet deep, which was a bit out of proportion for the size of the castle Kelsey was building.

"Maybe the moat should be a little shallower," I suggested. Tracy agreed.

The moat had steps in it so that the water would fall going around the moat. We worked on the castle for two hours, building a door and a drawbridge on the ocean side. Finally, we finished the entire project. Tracy and Kelsey started running back and forth to the sea getting buckets of water to fill the moat. As soon as they poured the water in, it disappeared into the sand.

"I think we're going to have trouble filling the moat," Kelsey concluded. "We still need a flag for the castle."

I found a stick and the bottom of a blue beach sandal. I tied the sandal to the stick and planted the blue flag in the corner turret. We also found two boats someone built out of sections of coconuts. The boats were placed inside the castle in case it flooded and the occupants needed to escape.

Paul came back from his shell hunt and agreed the moat should be a dry moat. He found two more starfish to go with the one he had back at the apartment. The starfish were two or three inches long. He also found a sea cucumber, an octopus and more beautiful shells for his collection.

The grandchildren decided to play tennis after lunch. None of them had ever played before, but that didn't dampen their juvenile enthusiasm. Kelsey had a great deal of trouble hitting the ball. She would swing below it every time. She eventually hit a few balls back to the net. Tracy and Paul faired better. I would lob the ball over the net and they would try to return it. We played for an hour--good exercise.

We walked back to the beach late in the afternoon.

"Grandpa! The ocean covered our castle with water," Tracy yelled. The tide had come in.

Kelsey accepted the fate--easy come, easy go. She and Tracy ran and jumped into the surf. They waded out waist-deep. The waves were two- or three-feet high. Every time a wave came in, the girls jumped into it. At first Kelsey was afraid to get her head underwater, but after half-a-dozen large waves it didn't bother her any more. They kept edging out deeper and deeper until they were up to their necks and the waves were washing over their heads. I called them back to shallower water and they would drift out to the deeper again. This was the first time Kelsey had played in the waves. She really enjoyed herself.

Port Douglas is a sleepy, little resort town at the end of a palm-lined peninsula. The town has more golf courses, resorts, marinas and beaches than people. On Thursday morning I rented bikes and the grandchildren and I rode four miles to the Port Douglas shopping district. The two-block long shopping area contained two-dozen stores, three restaurants and the post office. We stopped by the post office to buy the first day cover stamps featuring the bunyip. The bunyip is a mythical Australian animal that lives in the swamps. It is mischievous, and if anything is missing--your hairbrush, the dog, a broom--the bunyip is blamed. One of the tourist stores had a beautiful Barrier Reef shell collection consisting of several thousand shells. Paul checked it over and pointed out the shells he had in his collection.

After shopping and a refreshing soft drink, we biked to the Mirage Marina. The marina had a little sugarcane train that went from the docks out into the countryside and back. We stopped at their snack bar for some mint chocolate chip ice cream.

Our next stop was the Rainforest Habitat, a 100-acre park with birds, butterflies, kangaroos, koalas and crocodiles in their natural surroundings.

"Look at the big crocodiles!" Kelsey shouted as we crossed a wooden bridge over a pond containing a dozen huge crocodiles. The biggest crocodile opened its jaws and snapped at another that was invading his territory.

"Wow! They look hungry," Tracy said.

The kangaroo and wallabies were so tame we could walk up to them. Tracy and Kelsey petted a little wallaby that was dozing in the grass. It raised its head and looked around as the girls scratched its ears.

There were several koalas in the trees, but they sleep during the day. They did scratch their backside and move around a little, but never appeared to wake up.

"There's a thousand butterflies in here," Kelsey said when we entered the screened butterfly enclosure. An iridescent-blue tropical butterfly landed on Kelsey's yellow shirt and then took off when it couldn't find any nectar.

Paul brushed his head on something hanging from a tree branch as we left the butterfly enclosure and crossed a wooden bridge.

"Yikes!" Paul yelled.

He was eyeball-to-eyeball with a huge, furry fruit bat. The bat hung upside down from a branch. Its head was the size of a tennis ball and its wings spanned two feet or more. The bat was sleeping, but it opened its eyes and glared at Paul as if to ask, "Why are you bothering me?" Then it closed its eyes and covered its head with a wing. Paul didn't hang around to answer the question.

We biked down to a beach in Port Douglas to go swimming. The water at this beach was deep close in and the waves broke right by the shore. The wind was strong and the waves were big; about five-feet high with one wave arriving every five seconds. We played in the waves for an hour. The game was to try to stand up as these huge waves crashed into us. Kelsey tried to jump up when the waves came in, but they washed right over the top of her.

CHAPTER 14

THE TRIP HOME

The alarm was set for 3 a.m., but I woke up every 30 minutes all night long to check the clock. I was worried we'd oversleep and miss our flight. We were scheduled to catch the Coral Coach back to the Cairns airport at 4 a.m. The airlines were booked solid and if we missed our flight, we might not be able to reach Sydney in time to catch our scheduled flight to the U.S.

Three a.m. finally came and I got up after a restless night. Trying to wake and dress three exhausted grandchildren in the middle of the night was the next chore. They kept falling over. I'd stand one up and another one would fall back in bed. While Gloria finally finished dressing them, I packed the suitcases and we all stumbled out to the road to wait for the coach.

The cold morning air woke everyone up. While we waited we looked for constellations in the clear night sky.

"There's Orion rising in the East," I said.

"I see the Southern Cross," Tracy said.

"Is that the Magellanic Cloud they were telling us about at Ayers Rock?" Paul asked.

"Yeah, I think it is."

"I can't find the Big Dipper or the North Star anywhere," Kelsey said.

"We're too far south to see them."

At 4 a.m. the coach arrived, right on schedule. The grandchildren slept during the dark ride to the airport.

Shortly after dawn, our Ansett flight took off for Sydney. The first portion of the flight was over the Great Barrier Reef at 25,000 feet. It was like a private sight-seeing tour. Several hundred individual coral reefs or islands appeared below us, each

148

with its unique shape. They looked so blue and pristine from five miles up. Next, the aircraft passed over the rain forest. Hundreds of miles of solid tropical vegetation with no visible roads or fields. About 500 miles south of Cairns, the terrain changed to arid, barren land with huge farming areas and a few small, serpentine rivers flowing into man-made reservoirs.

Occasionally a green oasis with a golf course could be seen. There was a joke going around Australia that the Japanese wanted to buy all of Queensland and turn it into one giant golf course. The joke was based on fact since in the 1980s and early 1990s, Japanese companies were buying large tracks of "worthless" desert in Queensland and building golf resorts. The Japanese companies chartered a plane, filled it with their people and flew them to the resort. The holiday was totally orchestrated. The tourists were bused on sight-seeing trips aboard Japanese buses, ate at Japanese restaurants and shopped at Japanese stores. None of the tourist-related money went into the local economy--all was captured by the Japanese companies.

Our only stop was in Brisbane, the site of the 1994 World Games. It is a medium-sized city on the ocean with dozens of skyscrapers. South of Brisbane the land appeared very dry and brown, criss-crossed with roads leading to many small townships. Several grass and forest fires burned out of control. Apparently they let the fires burn themselves out as we could see no fire-fighting equipment or people working the fires.

Sydney appeared out the window around noon. After landing and collecting our luggage, we caught the bus to the Sydney Park Inn in Hyde Park. Sydney is a very comfortable city that reminded me of New Orleans. Rows of neat, older houses lined the streets. Many of the houses have elaborate wrought-iron porch railings and decorative trim. The city is divided into neighborhoods with their own ethnic culture and appearance. It doesn't feel like a big city.

149

Many of the houses in Sydney have wrought-iron porch railings.

Our apartment was right in the center of the city--very convenient. It consisted of two one-bedroom apartments joined together. After a short cat-nap, we walked to Darling Harbor to see the sights.

Darling Harbor was Sydney's first commercial harbor. As newer harbors took over the business of shipping, Darling was converted to a park, mall and entertainment center. We walked past 200 shops, a dozen restaurants, museums and gardens.

"Can we ride the monorail?" Paul asked.

We caught the monorail on Harbor Street and rode past the Chinese Gardens. The monorail traveled above the business district, giving us a bird's-eye view of the city.

"Look at the giant tower," Kelsey said, pointing to the 1,000-foot-high Sydney Tower with its revolving restaurant on top.

"There's the aquarium," Tracy said as the monorail crossed Cockle Bay.

We passed the huge Novetel hotel complex and passed over the Darling Harbor convention center exhibition area. About 30 minutes from the start we were back at Harbor Street Station, completing the 14-mile ride.

From there, we took a bus to Circular Quay and walked to the Sydney Opera House. The Opera House totally fills the narrow neck of land stretching from the Royal Botanical Gardens into Sydney Harbor.

"Is it made from seashells?" Kelsey asked when she saw the white, shell-shaped building.

"No. It's covered with white ceramic tiles made in Sweden--over a million of them."

"Looks like they couldn't decide when to stop building," Paul commented on the multi-roofed structure.

"It took 20 years to build," I said. "Originally they budgeted $12 million. The final cost was $102 million, paid for

151

The magnificent opera house is the symbol of Sydney.

by the Opera lottery. The building houses a concert hall, an opera theater, a drama theater and a music room. Even the wood in the seats was specially chosen to provide the best acoustical properties."

"It sure is pretty," Kelsey said. We all agreed.

The next morning we caught the ferry to the Sydney's Taronga Park Zoo. The view of the single-arch Coat Hanger Bridge towering over the harbor was spectacular from the ferry. We also passed by Fort Denison in the harbor, which had been a military prison. It was as difficult to escape from as Alcatraz-- cold water, strong currents and sharks discouraged escape attempts.

"Can we ride the cable car?" Kelsey asked as we disembarked from the ferry and started up the hill to the zoo.

"Sure," I said. The aerial tram carried us up the hill from the ferry dock and over the zoo. We had a bird's-eye view of the zoo which helped orient us to the layout.

The first exhibit we visited consisted of a nighttime display of nocturnal animals.

"There are those giant bats I ran into," Paul said as he pointed to the bats with a three-foot wingspan flying around their cage. In the dim light they looked like Dracula's vampires.

Next, we saw the koalas. Four koalas were sitting in short tree stumps in an enclosure. The attendant allowed a few people at a time (in this case, just our family) into the enclosure. We walked up, petted the koalas and took their picture.

The zoo staff had rearranged the koalas' body clocks. They turned the lights on in the koalas' enclosure at night so they would sleep, and kept the enclosure semi-dark during the day so they would be awake. The koalas were active, eating eucalyptus sprouts and frolicking around. A baby koala was riding on the caretaker's back. Did the baby think the caretaker was its mother? It clung to her as she walked around feeding the rest of the koalas.

The Apostle birds were busy chattering in their cage. These birds are dark gray and about the size of a dove. We had seen their mud nests in the trees where the birds lived in Rainbow Valley, but didn't get a close look at them until now.

The saltwater crocodiles were huge--about 30-feet long. I'd hate to meet one in the wild. They also had an albino crocodile--all white. It had a ghostly look to it. Probably wouldn't last long in the wild.

"Let's watch the seals," Kelsey said. We sat down and watched the performing seal show. They balanced balls on their noses, retrieved Frisbees from the water and, on command, slid down a slide into the pool. When the attendant gave them a fish as a reward, the seals clapped.

After the seal show, we walked through the kangaroo enclosure. The kangaroos and wallabies ignored us. We were within arm's reach of them, but they just dozed or went on eating.

The Taronga zoo had a nice collection of big cats. There were white tigers, snow leopards, black panthers, ocelots, pumas and Bengal tigers displayed in glass enclosures. The cats appeared to be curious about the visitors. They came very close to the glass and stood there nose-to-nose inspecting us while we got a close look at them.

We also saw dingoes, emus and a duck-billed platypus. The platypus is sure a strange animal. It looks like a muskrat with a duck bill and webbed feet. They lay eggs, but suckle their young. The platypus is equally at home on land or in the water.

The Tasmanian devil is a mean-looking animal; big teeth and long claws. They are known for their bad disposition. One theory suggests their hostility is due to a bad case of constipation.

Kelsey decided she wanted to take home a set of Australian coins so we sorted out all of my coins on the floor of the apartment after we returned from the zoo.

"There is a koala coin, kangaroos, crocodiles, platypus, sheep and a horse. Why not a camel?" Kelsey asked.

"I don't know. Maybe we should write the Prime Minister and suggest they mint a camel coin."

"That's a good idea," Kelsey agreed.

It took 24 hours to fly home from Sydney to Dayton. However, since we crossed the international dateline, we arrived home the same day we left Australia. The flight was just like the rest of the trip--*magic!*

"Did you have a good time?" Judy asked Kelsey at the airport.

"Yeah! You should have seen how fast my camel could run, and the big sandcastle we built."

REFERENCES

Berndt, R.M. & C.A., <u>The World of the First Australians</u>, Aboriginal Studies Press, Camberra ACT Australia, 1964 (revised 1988).

Caust, Peter, <u>Coober Pedy</u>, Brown & Associates, Carina, Queensland, Australia, 1989.

Davidson, Robyn, <u>Tracks</u>, Random House Australia, Sydney, New South Wales, Australia, 1980

Fahey, Warren, <u>When Mable Laid The Table</u>, State Library of New South Wales Press, Sydney, New South Wales, Australia, 1992.

Finlay, Hugh, <u>Northern Territory</u>, Lonely Planet Publications, Hawthorn, Victoria, Australia, September 1996.

Hardy, Frank, <u>Yarns of Billy Borker</u>, Mandarin Australia, Port Melbourne, Victoria, Australia, 1965.

Harney, Bill, <u>To Ayres Rock And Beyond</u>, Ian Drakefors Publishing, Byswater, Victoria, Australia, 1988

Hasluck, P., <u>Black Australians</u>, Melbourne University Press, Melbourne Australia, 1942.

Hayes, Mike, <u>Yarns From All Round Australia</u>, ABC BOOKS, Sydney, New South Wales, Australia, 1993.

155

Herrnstein, R.J, & C. Murray, The Bell Curve, Free Press, New York NY, 1994.

Keneally, T., Outback, Hodder & Stoughton, Lone Cove NSW Australia, 1983.

Johnson, Marael, Outback Australia Handbook, Moon Publications Inc, Chico CA, May 1992.

Whitlock, G. & D. Carter, Images of Australia, Univ of Queensland Press, St Lucia Queensland Australia, 1992.

INDEX

Books By Allen Johnson

[] AUSTRALIA FROM THE BACK OF A CAMEL

The 12 camels plodded through Rainbow Valley in the Australian outback. Kelsey, the author's 7-year-old granddaughter, nudged her 1,000-pound camel in the belly and Charcoal charged off in a cloud of dust, galloping to the head of the line. The author and 3 of his grandchildren were on a 7-day camel safari in the middle of the Australian desert. They spent 8 hours a day riding camels in search of caves with Aboriginal paintings, fossils, desert animals and unusual flora and fauna. At night the Johnsons slept on the ground around a huge fire to ward of the near-freezing temperature. They encountered wallabies, kangaroos, wedge-tailed eagles, dingos, emus and a variety of desert birds, lizards, snakes and spiders. The best part of the trip: "Running the camels across the dry lake-bed," Kelsey said. $16.95

[] BIKING ACROSS THE DEVIL'S BACKBONE

A 9-year-old and her grandfather pedaled 600 miles across the mid-West in search of adventure. Enroute they explored Cave-in-Rock on the Ohio River, the Garden of the Gods in southern Illinois, visited an ostrich farm in Mt. Vernon, spent the night with the monks at St. Meinrad Monastery, toured Lincoln's boyhood home in southern Indiana and pedaled over the razorback Devil's Backbone. Tracy maintained her good humor and high spirits while pedaling up to 65 miles a day through the hilly route in 95 degree heat. The best part of the trip? "The day at the monastery," replied Tracy. "Spending time with my granddaughter," explained Allen. $15.95

[] OUABACHE ADVENTURE-CANOEING THE WABASH

An adventure-packed 500-mile long trip canoeing down the Wabash River with the author and his 10-year-old grandson. From Fort Recovery, Ohio, they dragged the canoe through the shallow, upper Wabash, fought raging rapids and survived a 14-hour long thunder-lightening storm. At night the pair camped and fished along the banks of the river. They encountered deer, raccoons, muskrats,

162

rabbits, beaver, gars and pileated woodpeckers during their 16-day journey along the still-wild river. After paddling one-quarter-million strokes they finally reached their destination--the Ohio River. $13.95

[] DRIVE THROUGH RUSSIA? IMPOSSIBLE!

In 1981, the author and his wife rented a car and drove 4,000 miles through the Communist Soviet Union by themselves. This book describes the 3-week odyssey through the ancient countryside and modern bureaucracy. When the Johnsons first entered the Soviet Union, the officials informed them they would be staying the in the Pribaltiskaya Hotel that night in Leningrad. "What is the name of our hotel in Novgorod tomorrow night?" Allen asked. "It is not necessary for you to know. Tomorrow we will tell you where you will be staying." The author found that in the Soviet Union, information was power and the officials were very reluctant to give it away.   With a basic understanding of the Russian language learned from 3 years of tutoring in Dayton before the trip, the Johnsons traveled from town to town, purchased food and gasoline, interpreted the meager road maps and visited with the Russian people. They found the people curious, kind and helpful. Travel with the Johnsons and enjoy a vivid picture of their daily discoveries, pleasures and frustrations. $10.95

Order With This Convenient Coupon

Creative Enterprises
1040 Harvard Blvd.
Dayton OH 45406-5047

Please send me the books I have checked above. I am enclosing $_____ (please add $2.00 per book for postage/handling. Ohio residents add 6.5% tax). Send check or money order. You can also order from the internet. **http://www.creative-enterprises.org**
Name_____

Address_____

City_____ State _____ Zip Code _____

Allow 2--4 weeks for delivery.